VINTAGE DENIM

DENIM

By
DAVID LITTLE
Photographs by
LARRY BOND

GIBBS·SMITH
P
PUBLISHER

SALT LAKE CITY

First Edition
99 98 97 96 5 4 3 2 1

This is a Peregrine Smith Book, published by
Gibbs Smith, Publisher
P.O. Box 667
Layton, Utah 84041

Jacket design by Kinara Graphics, Thomas E. Berry
Book design and production by J. Scott Knudsen
Edited by Gail Yngve

Printed and bound in China

Library of Congress Cataloging-in-Publication Data
Little, David, 1953-
Vintage Denim / written by David Little; photographed by Larry Bond.
    p.   cm.
    ISBN 0-87905-664-9
1. Jeans (Clothing)—Collectors and collecting—United States.
2. Denim—Collectors and collecting—United States. 3. Vintage
clothing—Collectors and collecting—United States. I. Bond,
Larry, 1953- . II. Title.
GT2085.L58   1995
687—dc20   95-11531
                         CIP

For Mom and Dad,

who put me in my

first pair of jeans

ACKNOWLEDGEMENTS

Sometimes things happen that if you knew how hard it was going to be, you never would have done it. Such is the case with this book. Miraculously though, here it is. When I was first asked to write this book, it seemed a simple enough task, but without the contributions, help, and generosity of a lot of people who first incredulously asked, "A book about what?" this book never would have come together.

Thanks go to many but primarily to my friend and professional photographer Larry Bond whose skill and artistic eye was exceeded only by his patience as we proceeded without a map on the denim trail. That patience kept us out of jail when you didn't beat the hell out of that obnoxious guy who really had it coming at the Rose Bowl flea market. Thanks, Larry, for putting on the hats of creative director, art director, prop manager, makeup artist, driver, and critic. Thanks also to your wife and kids for understanding.

Thanks to all those who so generously and thoughtfully gave of their time, knowledge, enthusiasm, resources, props, collections, talents, skills, spare bedrooms, and cold beers.

This book would not have been possible without the cooperation of many denim dealers and collectors who were generous in sharing their love of old denim and many prized vintage-denim garments and advertising items with us. Special thanks to the following: Ron and Cynthia Wright and the staff at BOSS Unlimited in Denver, Colorado, who gave us the run of the place and many leads, tips, and information; Nihat Ulusoy, his brother, and staff at Worn Out West/American Vintage in Hollywood, California, who let complete strangers run amok in their great Melrose Avenue shop and even loaned us their sales staff as models; Barbara Dryden and her Mr. Higgin's Second Chance Vintage clothing store in Missoula, Montana, who gave me encouragement and a piece of the action on a pair of 1937 buckle-back Levi's; and Barbara's daughter Raven for lending a smile. Thanks to John Farley and his staff at Farley Enterprises and the *Vintage Partner* magazine for the use of their collection and expertise in preparing the price guide that accompanies this book; Jack Dovan of American Classics in Hollywood; Theodore Kyriaziz of Jethro Classic Wear, Los Angeles; and Marshal Sven Larson, Swede and owner of Marshall's Precious Metals, Incorporated. A very big thank you to Roy Rogers— Happy Trails! Thanks for the memories: Dusty Rogers, Roy Rogers, and Dale Evans Museum in Victorville, California; Gene Autry; Alex Gordon, vice president of Flying A Pictures, representing Gene Autry; the Gene Autry Western Heritage Museum; Raven Beauty Tattoos in Denver; John Sawazki of the Motor Ranch in Denver, Colorado, who gave us access to his extensive collection of motorcycles and motorcycle-related materials; Ken Fidler of the

Gallery of Cars in Denver for use of his James Dean Porsche Speedster (for a photo of it, anyway); Vinnie Terranova of Rocky Mountain Harley Davidson; Willie G. Davidson, director of Styling at Harley-Davidson Motor Company, Inc. in Milwaukee; and Harley-Davidson's company archivist and historian, Dr. Martin Jack Rosenblum. Thanks also to Harley-Davidson's Karen Davidson and Kerri Martin; the Denver Police Department; Walt Swanson and his great old vehicles; The Forney Transportation Museum in Denver, Colorado, for use of their trains; Karen Michelson at the Chicago Urban Outfitters for allowing us to photograph the store; Boogie's Diner in Chicago and Aspen for allowing us the use of their stores for backdrops; Sleeper Antiques, Denver, Colorado, for their great props; Dan and Bill, old pals who let us camp in their West Hollywood home, and then took all our money in a crooked poker game (because we were tired and had a few margaritas and beers in us); Bob Weiglein and Kate, good friends and the best Chicago thrift-store guides. (Some fun, eh, Bob?); Elizabeth Clair Flood, fellow Gibbs Smith author—thanks for the call and the advice; Gary Schneckloth who allowed us heathens into his basement shrine to Roy Rogers to photograph his amazing cowboy collection; David Metcalfe for use of his great record collection; Maria Tessmer and her twins Sam and Alex for their cute faces; Debbie Shea and Teresa Yung for modeling; Nelli and Monica at the John Robert Powers International Model Agency in Denver and the patient and generous models they provided for our photographs.

For help in research, thank you to Levi Strauss and Company and their archivist and historian, Lynn Downey, for help in researching the facts of this manuscript; Wrangler and their historian Linda Hand at the Wrangler Archives in Greensboro, North Carolina, for her help, research, and loan of archival material—thanks to her staff and volunteers, too; H. D. Lee Company and Lee historian and archivist, Claudia Broadus, and her staff in Merriam, Kansas.

To my brother and my sister Cat who first taught me how to look "cool" in jeans and to taper those tight ones back in 1967.

To my patient editor and new friend Gail Yngve at Gibbs Smith, Publisher, who crowned me the King of Ellipsis and fought to make this book one I could put my name on. Thanks for keeping us out of jail in Orem, Utah.

To Gibbs Smith, who took on this project and who has greater vision for books than I do. Thanks, Gibbs. Yes, it really was interesting.

To Lana Perrotti for her encouragement, patience, creative input, editing, modeling skills, food and drink for the crew. Thanks for your computer expertise and patience with the novice and for being an unconditional pal while I finished this book. Thanks, Hon!

To everyone we didn't have room to list who really helped this project along, THANKS!!

CONTENTS

INTRODUCTION

Denim. Jeans. America is a country that prides itself on its toughness, individuality, and youthful spirit; it is difficult to find a common thread woven through time that has remained unchanged and as popular or durable as jeans made of cotton denim.

In this land of individualists and freedom-loving freethinkers, there has never been a uniform that clothed that individuality; but if there had been, it would have been the American-made blue denim jeans.

For more than 140 years, blue jeans have lived to express what Americans have believed themselves to be—strong, unpretentious, unadorned, informal, comfortable, classless, hardworking, reliable, and consistent, improving with time. The writer of an *Esquire* magazine article even called denim blue jeans "America's second skin." If there is a universal uniform of individuality, it is blue jeans: an article of clothing, not a fashion item, that appeals to all ages, professions, occupations, political persuasions, sizes, and nationalities. Blue jeans are a universal language, understood in almost every country around the world, and manufactured and worn in almost every corner of the world.

What makes denim so appealing? There is a comfort in the continuity of blue jeans. They are something to count on in a rapidly and ever-changing world. The classic American blue jeans remain virtually unchanged in more than a hundred years. It is a rare thing in American culture to find anything loved for its sameness. In a youth-oriented, future-thinking society, there is precious little Americans can appreciate and count on to remain the same that actually gets better with age and wear. We are attracted to newness but retain a fondness for "oldness."

We know we can always get another pair of blue jeans. And we know that, for the most part, they will be just like the pair we had before, and the pair before that, and on and on and on.

Buying a new pair of blue jeans is almost rebirth. We may never have another dog like the one we loved and lost, or another romance like the one that grew and died, but we can always get another pair of jeans.

Like a tattoo, denim jeans have become a part of us, almost like a second skin.

RadioTimes

CLINT EASTWOOD
—director—
As BBC2's 'Arena' makes your Friday, meet
the star behind the camera

Stars such as
actor/director Clint
Eastwood can afford to
wear anything they want,
but simple, comfortable
denim is the garment of
choice for many
Hollywood celebrities.

Jeans are a common denominator—a great equalizer. Maybe we can't afford the houses, cars, and lifestyles of the rich and famous, but we can wear the same jeans rock stars and Hollywood celebrities wear. And we can wear them forever. Blue jeans are an expression of youth that we can wear for a lifetime. We don't ever grow out of jeans; we grow into them.

Blue jeans made of blue-indigo-dyed cotton are an American classic: one of the rare, truly American contributions made to the fashion history of the world. So little is "purely American," but blue jeans are on the list, right along with jazz, baseball, cowboys, and rock 'n' roll.

Before jeans became an American classic, they were just a simple, sturdy style of pants invented by Levi Strauss for the miners of the California gold rush as the first denim clothing in the United States. By the turn of the century, the "two-horse" brand, as Levi's are often known, had become synonymous with strong, rugged clothing. They were destined to become a legend with the working men and women who first wore them. Jeans were not yet considered sexy; they were associated with strength. Jeans were not yet stylish; they were simply sturdy.

DENIM BECOMES COLLECTIBLE

How was the leap from strong and sturdy to sexy and chic accomplished? Why did something so commonplace come to be collectible, so valuable or rare that it might bring thousands of times its original cost? What is this mystique surrounding a plain blue pair of pants or a jacket that suddenly has frantic dealers and collectors throwing ever-growing fistfuls of dollars toward those lucky enough to own a "vintage denim" garment? (Usually vintage denim is denim considered to be at least twenty years old.) Who is buying these "old clothes" anyway, and how in the world could an old denim jacket from the 1920s suddenly be worth upwards of $15,000? Has the hunger for things "truly American" become so insatiable that Europeans and Asians have raised the rank of old blue jeans to icon status?

Seen strictly from a coldhearted, mercenary point of view, it all boils down to money. A market has been created, and the buying and selling of vintage denim clothing is making some people rich. Vintage denim (old jeans and jeans jackets, primarily) as an international commodity is a relatively new phenomenon. Most fortunes made in this strange business have been made in the past fifteen years. During the 1970s, somewhat of a black market for American-made Levi's blue jeans existed, but the demand was for contemporary jeans, mostly button-fly Levi 501s. Some savvy sellers of denim actually financed their travels through Europe and Russia in those days by selling Levi's.

But the interest in buying, selling, and collecting vintage or antique denim clothing is a fairly recent phenomenon. No one seems to know whether it was a fad just waiting to happen or a plan carefully contrived by a few to create a demand they were ready to supply.

Levi Strauss and Company is the largest apparel manufacturer in the world and the second largest jeans maker in the United States behind Vanity Fair, or VF Corporation,

This vintage Levi Strauss and Company advertising piece explains some of the popularity of Levi's jeans. The slogan "Fits 'Em All" was a reference to the comfort and adaptability of denim pants referred to as "America's Finest Overall" in its early years.

which now owns Wrangler, Lee, and Rustler brands of jeans clothing. Levi Strauss and Company has about 40,000 domestic retail outlets in the United States, to say nothing of outlets in other countries. The company estimates it has sold 2.5 billion pairs of jeans in its history. Obviously, hundreds of pairs of Levi's—to say nothing of other brands produced since 1870—are out there in the world. They couldn't possibly be so rare or valuable to have become equal in status to a rare antique or vintage automobile, could they?

This banner at the Rose Bowl in Pasadena, California, proclaims to buyers that this flea market is a mecca for vintage-denim dealers and collectors.

THE JAPANESE CONNECTION

A visit to one of many vintage denim collectors and dealers along Los Angeles's Melrose Avenue, Tokyo's Shibuya Park area, flea markets such as the Rose Bowl in Pasadena, California, or a boutique in Paris make it clear that it's true. Vintage denim is a "hot" collectible, one that has shown no signs of cooling off in the past fifteen years. What do collectors know that the rest of us don't, and why couldn't most of us see what was

Early in the morning, buyers sort through the tons of vintage and collectible denim for sale at the Rose Bowl.

happening? The Smithsonian Institute in Washington, D.C., added a pair of Levi's 501s to its permanent collection more than thirty years ago. An estimated 2,000 tons of vintage and contemporary American-made jeans are shipped to Japan every year, and the amount has been growing steadily. But, besides dealers and collectors in the business to make money, mainstream America has been slow to catch on to this phenomenon. And why not? After all, to most American consumers jeans are jeans—a pair of Levi's is a pair of Levi's, a pair of Wrangler's is a pair of Wrangler's—it doesn't really matter if they were made in 1940 or yesterday. They seem to be, on the surface at least, the same good ol' jeans we grew up in and with. From the jeans we wore as children, with the gooey ironed-on knee patches, to the pegged and tapered jeans of junior high, to the painted and studded jeans of the sixties, to the acid-washed, bleached, distressed, ripped, and cut jeans of the eighties, and finally, to the pressed designer jeans of the nineties—weren't they, in effect, all the same? Most wearers weren't discriminating enough to see the difference between the jeans their fathers wore from those worn today.

The denim sellers were just as enamored with jeans as the masses were, yet they had the vision to see them as something more than just another pair of pants. With that vision, they helped to create a market in which an old blue jeans jacket may well be worth more than a full-length mink coat.

Such a man of vision is Kenji Hirano, owner of Banana Boat, one of many Shibuya Street vintage denim shops in Tokyo. According to Cynthia Wright of Boss Unlimited, a large vintage denim and clothing wholesaler and retailer in Denver, Colorado, Kenji was one of the founding fathers and creators of the trend in Japan for wearing vintage American denim. Many others

probably can claim the title of "founding father," but Kenji was certainly among the first in Japan. In the United States, vintage clothing was beginning to be something more than "used clothes," but still, the prevailing attitude towards wearing used clothing was that is was only something for poor people who couldn't afford new clothes.

Twenty years ago, Kenji was living in Hawaii and exporting older Volkswagen "Beetles" and Karmann Ghias to Japan. He noticed a strong appreciation for things old and things American there and thought blue jeans were as strong a symbol of the

American culture as, say, a Harley-Davidson motorcycle but at a price much more affordable and attractive to Japanese young people.

Kenji began a series of travels across the back roads of America. Armed with a road atlas and a great idea, he took off on his "dead stock tour" of America. "Dead stock" is how professional vintage buyers refer to old, unsold merchandise that a store might have had put away in a basement or warehouse for many years—in some instances, for many, many years. Along Melrose Avenue in Hollywood, there are some vintage stores that deal only in dead stock, or, as it is sometimes

Like something stamped "sterling" or "18 carat gold," the leather label of a vintage pair of Levi's 501s Double Xs is a recognized mark of value to vintage-denim buyers and collectors.

At a California swap meet, a cutout paper figure of American icon James Dean points to another American icon— a vintage pair of Levi Strauss jeans made in a huge size to serve as an advertising piece in the 1950s.

called, "new old stock." These are items that might be ten, fifteen, or even forty years old but still like new, the original tags and labels intact, but for some reason the item never sold.

It would seem to most that a store dealing only in dead stock would soon be out of business. But, according to Jack Dovan, owner of American Classics, a vintage store on Melrose Avenue in West Hollywood, "There is a huge amount of stuff out there." Still, Jack told me that back in 1983, and now, twelve years later, most would say "things have changed." According to Ron and Cynthia Wright at Boss, fifteen years ago when people such as Kenji started collecting, "almost no one" was interested in vintage denim, and Kenji was often the first person ever to visit the warehouses, storerooms, basements, and back rooms of many stores across America.

Some of Kenji's blue jeans odysseys took as long as six months, but a warehouse in Los Angeles and another one in Tokyo, often brimming with the "blue gold" of vintage denim, was the payoff for all the road miles, truck-stop food, and rummaging through dark, musty basements. I'm sure Kenji left many an old storekeeper in the Midwest shaking his head in disbelief that this crazy Japanese guy just gave him good money for a bunch of worthless clothes that he couldn't sell in thirty years. Kenji has an article from a small-town Texas newspaper with a picture of him and a huge pile of old stock denim, the headline reading "Japanese Raid Local Store."

THE CONTROVERSY

Japan is raiding us, according to some of the more sensitive dealers and jealous competitors who feel Americans are selling and Japanese are buying an important piece of our American heritage. Never mind that very few Americans ever thought about buying up all that dusty old denim; to many Americans this was an act of pillage, when foreigners were once again plundering the gems of our past and hauling them out of the country.

As old Harley-Davidson and Indian motorcycles are restored, crated, and shipped overseas, as buyers from Europe and Asia comb America's flea markets, auctions, and antique stores for cowboy gear to take back home, many people feel Americans are selling off their roots. As one of the youngest countries in the world, are our short history and its historical artifacts worth nothing more than the dollars overseas buyers are willing to pay? Some claim Americans only get interested in the pieces from their past when there is a buck to be made selling those pieces.

It is the sad history of the world that countries have ransacked one another, plundering their treasures and artistic "souls." Following many wars, a victorious country may end up with more art, artifacts, and treasures of their vanquished foes than were left in the defeated country. But can something as common and mundane as a mass-produced

Without a printed word left on its wrinkled leather face, a vintage Levi's 501 tag is still recognizable and universally understood to say "this is a pair of Levi's."

With their roots coming from the humble beginnings of work clothing, denim jeans and jackets have become a universal uniform of comfortable and stylish fashion.

pair of pants or a denim jacket be compared to the true treasures of the world's art and literature? Probably not, but at least in Japan, the wearing and collecting of that blue bit of American history has been elevated to a new status. No one can really say why this has happened. It is, perhaps, simply a love affair with things American— something comfortable and informal in a country long on tradition and formality, a country where once only kimonos existed. In fact, in the early language of Japan, *kimono* meant "clothes" because that was all there was to wear.

During the occupation of postwar Japan, American GIs were the first to display casual wear to the Japanese, who were curious about these Americans, their strange language, informality, and perhaps, even those blue pants the Americans called jeans.

If given a chance, psychologists might come up with many deep and dark rationales for what appears to be, on the surface, a harmless and fun trend, a silly, youthful fad. They might point to the popularity of vintage (especially World War II) military aviator

clothing now being worn and collected in Japan. To those who survived the war years both in Japan and America, it may seem a bitter irony to see young Japanese wearing United States Navy G-1 or leather flight jackets from World War II.

Japan is an ancient country with a culture steeped for centuries in a strict code of tradition, honor, and respect. The Japanese have a long and rich history of a proud and civilized people, but often those traditions were reflected in a culture that did not honor individuality or individual expression. By tradition or out of respect, it was a culture that usually encouraged sameness and a tight uniformity among its people.

Perhaps this obsession with things American—which is such a young culture and country—is a response by Japanese youth who are eager to express their individuality and break away from some of the more traditional aspects of Japanese culture.

Maybe collecting things old and American is simply a status thing, an exhibition of wealth by young Japanese who may think nothing of spending hundreds of dollars for a 1960s pair of Levi's 501s. If, indeed, it isn't a status thing, then how have the value of various items of denim clothing come to be so distinct from one another? Why is one pair of old denim pants considered cool or hip in Japan while another seemingly similar pair is just a pair of old pants?

PRICING DENIM

Although there is no official price guide or "Blue Book" of values like there is for automobiles, guns, dolls, Zippo lighters, or just about any other collectible, there does exist among most dealers an unwritten pricing guide for almost all collectible and wearable denim, both vintage and contemporary. John Farley of Vintage Partners, one of the contributors to this book, has tried to demystify the vintage denim business and reveal, for the first time, some of the real prices denim can command overseas. By providing a price guide for this book, Farley hopes both buyers and sellers will be better informed as to the worth of their vintage clothing items.

As with any new hot collectible, the media usually prefers to report the gee-whiz factor. Usually, the gee-whiz factor has to do with the amazing amounts of money a certain collectible has brought on the open market. Such stories change the marketplace and often don't reflect the actual value of most collectibles but only a single, unusual item that sold for an unbelievable amount of money. Such is the case with vintage denim. When Paul Harvey broadcasts to America about old jeans bringing thousands of dollars, or an article in Vogue magazine (April 1995) touts vintage denim and prominently displays a $10,000 pair of Lee jeans, people begin to

All You Will Need Is a 36 Waist, A 33 Inseam and a Thick Wallet

By Carl Quintanilla
Staff Reporter of The Wall Street Journal

This is a story for those with deep pockets.

Cynthia and Ron Wright, a couple from Denver, have found what they say is the oldest pair of never-worn, never-washed Levi's jeans in the world. The pants appear to date back to 1927 or 1928. They are crisp and unfaded — and are now available for purchase, at a price acceptable to the Wrights.

The latest offer is $30,000.

The Wrights, who run a vintage-clothing store in Denver called Boss Unlimited, found the trousers (waist 36 inches, length 33 inches) this past May while stocking up on inventory. A man identifying himself as a retired salesman for Levi Strauss & Co. sold them the jeans for $2,500. He said he ran across them years ago and threw them in a drawer.

Since acquiring the venerable denim, the Wrights have been receiving offers that wouldn't be inappropriate for cloth of gold. A clothing collector offered $25,000 for the jeans. No sale. A clothing dealer from Japan flew into town recently and offered $30,000. Says Ms. Wright: "He laid them down on the floor and started touching them. He just went nuts." But the Wrights held out.

David Little, author of an upcoming book about jeans called "Vintage Denim," has seen the pants and says they are authentic. "They look like they just came off the rack," he says, but their antiquity is apparent in their suspender buttons and their "buckle back," an old-time device that allows the pants to be cinched without a belt.

The Wrights are keeping the jeans in a safe-deposit box and carrying them around in a secured attache case. They say they will keep their treasure until the end of the year while they consider new offers. Last weekend, more collectors flew in to look at, and bid on, the pants.

But at least one prospective buyer isn't planning to make an offer. "The price is way out of my ballpark," says Lynn Downey, Levi Strauss & Co.'s historian and blue-jean museum curator. "It's out of anybody's ballpark."

Ms. Wright thinks otherwise. She says the price may eventually get up to $75,000. That would be enough to send the Wrights' 13-year-old son, Jared, to medical school. "He wants to be a doctor," she says, laughing. "And we were wondering how we were going to pay for it."

take notice. Unfortunately, they have very little knowledge and assume any old pair of jeans can be the key to new riches. Most used jeans actually are just that—used jeans. There are millions of lottery tickets sold, but only a few actually are tickets to wealth. The same could be said for vintage denim.

Used-denim prices are not listed in the daily stock quotes of the Nikkei, Japan's stock exchange, nor do they appear on the New York Stock Exchange or the Paris or London markets. But an informal pricing code does exist, both for buying and selling. Of course, as with any collectible, an item's age, rarity, and condition dictate its value. Demand, as always, is the big measuring stick for setting prices. And that demand is a fickle and fast-changing commodity in Japan.

This article appeared in the Marketplace section of the *Wall Street Journal* front page, September 1995, proving that vintage denim has become a big business.

ment, the rarer it will be. If jeans were not worn to the threadbare state, cut off for summer shorts, or used for rags, they might be rare enough to have some value. But most Americans discard clothing well before it is worn out. Even with jeans, some people would discard them once they became too faded, to replace them with a new, bluer pair. Finding vintage denim in good shape is harder than might be expected. Even though a mass-produced item, there are some gems in the denim-collectible market that are rarely, if ever, found. Cynthia Wright tells of a 1940s Lee "Cowboy"-brand denim jacket that is presently on consignment in a shop in Tokyo. The owner of the jacket wants $6,000. Who knows what the jacket will eventually bring. Cynthia says in ten years of buying and selling denim, she has never seen "even one" of that particular jacket. A similar jacket, a dead-stock Levi's jacket from the early 1940s, reportedly sold at the Rose Bowl flea market recently for $5,000. Fortunes are being made in vintage denim. According to an article in the July 1994 *Esquire*, in 1992 at a Paris auction, eager buyers bid frantically on a Levi's promotional item from the 1930s, a pair of 501s on a cardboard cowboy. Bidding reportedly reached 130,000 francs, or about $75,000. Not coincidentally, denim is big business in the country of its humble origins. Recently, at the Palais Galliera at Paris's Fashion and Costume Museum, the French paid tribute to American classic blue jeans and other denim garments with an exhibit tracing the humble blue jeans from their beginnings to the haute couture items they've become. Curator Pascale Gorguet-Ballestros assembled the exhibit in her tribute to what fashion designer Christian Lacroix once called "the privileged vehicle for individual expression."

What is "in" one month may be "out" the next. For that reason, hoarding large inventories of any vintage item can be a costly mistake, and a seller's stock of high-demand vintage could only be worth the price of a rag in a rapidly changing market.

Certain vintage denim pieces may have a greater status and value as time goes on. How is the status of what you are wearing determined? How are the prices set for vintage denim? Why would a Japanese teenager, with his Levi's 501 blue jeans cuffs rolled up, showing barely visible "red stripes" of thread along the inseams, be worthy of more status and admiration than his friend, wearing a worn but newer pair of Levi's 501s? It's in the details mostly. And Japanese buyers know their details. Just as it is true with most any collectible, the older the better, and the more valuable. Because, logically, the older a gar-

Dramatic stories of high prices paid for lowly denim garments are the gems of the denim market, and the gem supply is quickly

Advertising items such as this Levi's Saddleman statue from the 1950s as well as vintage-denim garments have caught the eyes of collectors and now demand high prices.

drying up. Like finding a real Matisse or Monet painting at a garage sale, it doesn't happen every day. When it does, it's either blind luck, fate, or the finder has walked his shoes off in the search. As awareness increases of the value in vintage denim, more and more young Americans are digging through Dad's or Granddad's closet to find a vintage pair of jeans that could possibly be exchanged for enough cash to buy a secondhand car! Buyers and pickers scour the countryside, visiting thrift stores, flea markets, and garage sales in search of this elusive "blue gold."

"After fifteen years, most of the really easy-to-find, good vintage has dried up," according to Barbara Dryden, owner of Mr. Higgin's Second Chance Clothing in Missoula, Montana, and a denim buyer for more than ten years. It would seem that in the cowboy country of rural Montana, vintage denim jeans and jackets would appear daily at Dryden's shop where she specializes in buying used Levi's, but it's not so. "It's gotten so competitive," Barbara said. "There are many buyers here in Missoula alone [a town of about 75,000], and there are buyers who visit here on a regular basis and set up shop for a week or so and run 'WILL BUY LEVI'S' advertisements in the local newspapers." As the word gets out, Dryden says she turns away more potential sellers every day. "People have gotten the idea that anything worn and made of denim is worth money. You can't believe the rags people bring in to sell, thinking they have something of value."

Among those rags there is an occasional treasure. Barbara recently sold a pair of 1930s vintage, buckle-back Levi's that had never been washed. Eager first-level buyers gave her almost $2,000 for the pair of pants. What they ultimately will sell for after they change hands several times is hard to tell, but it will certainly make sorting through those denim rags worthwhile.

Vintage denim with labels still attached, such as these very early Blue Bell Wrangler jeans, can more easily date a vintage garment and raise the value considerably.

IDENTIFYING VALUABLE DENIM

If a person is not lucky enough to find a mint condition pair of buckle-back Levi's 501s from the thirties, how will he know if he has anything of value? According to most jeans buyers and wholesalers in this country, here's what to look for in order of value: anything denim (or marked Levi Strauss) from the 1880s to the 1950s. These items are getting so rare that brand, size, and condition, which normally would establish higher prices, are not always a consideration. The common attitude is, if it's really old, buy it. Ignore the holes, tears, and stains; buy it anyway. If it's really old and in mint condition, even better. "Mint condition" in this case means that that's probably close to what it

will bring in markets overseas. Perfect jeans and jackets, pre-1950s, are literally worth a mint as they become more scarce. The same goes for any denim-related products, advertising, or promotionals. These items, too, are getting to be worth more than their weight in gold in overseas markets.

Although there have been numerous jeans manufacturers, in the course of the last 130 years, most collectors limit themselves to the "Big Three" of denim clothing manufacturers: Levi, Lee, and Wrangler. Following Levi Strauss's success in the 1800s, H. D. Lee began making denim work clothing in the 1890s, and Blue Bell denim garments came on the market in the 1920s. That company spawned another denim giant with the Wrangler brand in the 1950s.

Today there are only two major jeans manufacturers in the United States. Levi Strauss and Company is the oldest manufacturer but is second in size and volume to the VF (Vanity Fair) Corporation that purchased Lee in 1969 and Wrangler (formerly Blue Bell) in 1986. These two companies alone produce about 90 percent of the domestic jeans brands sold in America. VF Corporation manufactures jeans under several different labels besides Wrangler and Lee.

Most denim collectors and sellers began with buying only Levi-brand denim—the Levi's 501 denim jeans and the Levi's blue-denim jacket represented the items: the older the better, and the more valuable in the eyes of most Japanese and European buyers. No matter that James Dean might have worn Lee jeans, Levi meant American blue jeans. But as older vintage Levi's became more scarce and as buyers became more sophisticated and knowledgeable, both Lee and Wrangler began to compete with the Levi denim, and rising prices reflected that interest.

If there is a gold standard in blue jeans, it

The H. D. Lee Company became the first real competition for Levi Strauss and Company when they began making denim work clothing in the 1890s.

is the Levi's 501 double-X, button-fly jeans. They are the oldest and have remained truest to the original jeans Levi Strauss made in the 1880s. But not all Levi's 501s were created equal, and there have been changes in the long evolution of the original 501s. After gaining rivets at "points of stress" back in 1873, the 501s lost a few of those rivets through some unique situations. One of the original stress points identified by Levi Strauss was the crotch of the jeans. That weak spot was remedied via a copper rivet stuck smack dab between the legs of the jeans. That single rivet was the source of much consternation (and some pain) to a multitude of Levi's wearers for almost seventy years. Numerous requests were made to the manufacturer to remove the cursed copper rivet with its unique heat-conducting properties. But it took a camping trip and a too-close campfire to finally convince then-Levi-president Walter Haas Sr. to make an executive decision to do away with the "branding iron" copper crotch rivet. It disappeared in the

1940s. A pair of Levi's with that rivet in the crotch is a truly valuable bit of denim history.

Back pocket rivets, a staple since the 1870s, also disappeared from the outside of the pants after Levi Strauss received many complaints from Levi's-wearing cowboys who were unhappy that those rivets were scratching the leather on their saddles. In addition, schools across the country implored Levi Strauss to do away with those metal rivets because students' riveted Levi's were wreaking havoc with the wooden chairs and desk seats in the classrooms. Those rivets disappeared from view in 1937 and were banished to the inside of the back pocket. Levi Strauss referred to these hidden rivets as "concealed copper rivets" until they disappeared altogether in the sixties when they were replaced by strong double stitching on the back pockets.

A simple copper rivet in the crotch or on the back pockets of a pair of vintage Levi's can bring the finder thousands of dollars today in Tokyo or Bangkok. Obviously, the existence of rivets in those two places can certainly help establish the vintage of an old pair of Levi's, but there are other clues that are not so obvious and some that are known mostly only to jeans-buying professionals and collectors.

A few other identifying marks exist, but as famous designer Coco Chanel once said, "Fashion changes. Style remains." So has it been with American denim, for the most part. Fashions have come and gone on the winds of whim and whimsy. American jeans and jeans jackets have style that has survived intact through the fickle and flimsy changes of fashion. The style of denim has strength and has endured with very little change since its humble beginnings.

In denim, it is the raw material, not the style, that has been most affected by time and history. The weight of denim has changed, from heavy to light to medium and back again numerous times. Denim manufacturers often used the weight of their material to set them apart from their competitors. Wars, economic fluctuations, consumer demand, fashion—all have played a part in the subtle changes of denim garments. Thread colors might change, size and color of rivets might change, buttons change, zippers change,

dyeing methods change, sewing methods change as technology progresses, but the style of jeans and jeans jackets is as close to constant as anything in the garment industry could ever be. A pocket might be added, a pleat taken away, a seam added, a lining added, a garment cut looser or made to fit tighter, but it is always recognizable for its true character. A person doesn't have to worry about buying doubles of a garment in fear she no longer can get the style she wants again. Denim was and is a classic.

Around the world, jeans became as common as Coca-Cola. But it is the subtle changes that denim garments have undergone over the years that have made them a valuable and sought-after collectible. The metamorphosis has not gone undetected. In this book, with the help of veteran vintage hunters, dealers, and collectors, some of the "secret" knowledge of these denim connoisseurs will be shared. Along the way, homage will be paid to those wonderful, soft, blue denim garments that have transcended simple form and function to become an American legend and an eternal symbol woven into the fabric of history.

Although Levi Strauss and Company has offered its 501 jeans in various colors over the years, these pants are an example of used 501s being overdyed in almost any color imaginable.

GOLD DUST AND DENIM
THE BEGINNINGS

Most people aren't thinking about history when they pull on or pull off a pair of denim jeans. They've other things on their minds—too much to realize that they are wearing something akin to living history. It's a testimony to the toughness of jeans that those worn today aren't a lot different from the first pairs—the denim britches that Levi Strauss first sewed together to cover the threadbare butts of early-day gold seekers during the California gold rush of 1849.

Joining the exodus from the East to the promise of a new El Dorado in California, a young traveling salesman named Levi Strauss came west hoping to make his fortune, too. He didn't come to join the multitudes clamoring for golden nuggets among the muck and mud of those early mines and gold camps; Strauss hoped to mine his gold from the pockets of the miners who were certain to need the canvas, needles, threads, scissors, and other materials he had brought with him from his family's dry goods business back

Miners such as these were the inspiration for young Levi Strauss to invent a pair of pants that could stand up to the rough use of gold mining.

east. Aboard his ship, fellow travelers with time on their hands and some money in their pockets bought up most of Strauss's supplies during the long voyage to California. He was left with a lot of heavy brown tent canvas, hoping to make tents for the hordes of homeless and hotel-less fortune hunters.

Most of the frenzied prospectors didn't care about tents. They were too busy digging and panning through the promise-laden California dirt and would often fall asleep right on the ground next to their "diggin's." They also didn't care about fashion. Most had arrived in the gold fields with the clothes on their backs—city clothes, which couldn't stand up to the rigors of hands and knees digging or panning and soon resembled rags. The knees and seats of their pants soon gave out, but a true gold digger, a real "forty-niner,"

Looking almost like a piece of paper currency, this oil cloth label from a 1930s pair of Levi's 501 Double X "Blue Denim Original Riveted Overalls" is as valuable as the money it resembles.

The father of the 501s, Levi Strauss probably never wore a pair of his denim overalls. But he created a tough, hard-wearing yet comfortable garment that has remained virtually unchanged for more than 140 years.

was no slave to fashion when there was gold to be found.

History and legend often tell different tales, but legend has it that a ragged miner in a bar (where most good legends begin) asked, or better, bet young Levi Strauss that he couldn't make a pair of pants to stand up to the rigors of gold mining. Whether there was really a wager or not, Strauss won by coming up with a pair of sturdy, functional pants fashioned from the durable cotton fabric he had hoped to make into tents and tarps. The young traveling salesman had found his own El Dorado. His riches came

out of the gold fields in the form of his waist-high overalls, as they were called, and became an instant hit with the bloody-kneed and needy forty-niners.

"The Birth of the Blues" came for young Levi Strauss when his pants became so popular he couldn't keep himself in canvas. That would always be true for Strauss's jeans, even in the next hundred years. Strauss originally imported canvas by the boatload from overseas. But that took too much time and the demand was immediate. The solution was to switch to a more readily available fabric that was still tough, durable, and comfortable enough for his demanding clientele. The fabric he switched to was denim, manufactured in a mill in New Hampshire but originally loomed and worn in the south of France and called *serge de Nîmes*, for the French town of Nîmes. The word "denim" has its roots here—from *de Nîmes* to denim. The other half of the universal "denim jeans," the word "jeans," supposedly also has its roots in the French language. Sailors from the Italian port of Genoa, or *Genes* in French, were some of the first to wear trousers made from this "denim" fabric. The color blue, for what would eventually be known throughout the world as

The classic Levi's button-fly jeans have been worn by millions since a miner put on the first pair in the California gold fields of the 1850s.

"blue jeans" denim, also came from the early French makers of denim.

Weavers in seventeenth-century Nîmes were dyeing their strong, light fabric an indigo color. This dark blue tint was made from the fermented leaves of the Indigofera plant, indigenous to China and India, and until German chemist Adolf von Baeyer created synthetic indigo dye in 1897, it was a completely natural, and somewhat rare, dye. Also, this natural blue dye often bled and created the famed "Blue Men" of the Arabian desert who wrapped themselves in indigo-dyed fabric to protect themselves from the relentless desert sun and stinging sand and wind. There are no reports of blue-legged miners during the dawn of denim along the California coast, but it probably happened. Another legend lost.

The new jeans were dark blue and stiff, but they were hard-wearing and softened with time. They weren't exactly tailor-made either, but the poor fit was often helped by a miner taking a soak in a nearby horse trough in his new Levi's, as the pants were beginning to be called. There were no belt loops, only suspender buttons and a waist-cinching buckle on the back such as those used to tighten a vest. They were strictly utilitarian pants—as plain as dirt—but at least the deep blue hid the grit, grease, and grime of a day's work. And they were strong. The pants became even stronger when, in 1872, a Nevada tailor, accustomed to building saddle blankets and other tack for horses using copper rivets, added those same rustproof rivets to a pair of Levi's pants. Legend again said that a miner had asked that tailor, Jacob Davis, to reinforce his Levi's pants pockets with rivets so he could carry more gold nuggets. The job done, Davis contacted his fabric supplier, Levi Strauss, and together they patented these riveted denim jeans. Prospectors could now stuff more ore into

their pockets without bursting the seams. And Levi began to stuff more miners' money into his pockets as well.

Despite their European origin of French material and names, the blue denim jeans were strictly American, and, almost overnight, an American success story. Strauss began to protect his success when in 1873 he added a trademark row of double orange stitching on the back pockets. Another legend went that the design symbolized the wings of an American eagle in flight. The stitching was the first nonfunctional aspect of the pants; it was just for decoration or, some say, a tribute to the American spirit represented by the dogged determinism and endless optimism of the early-day prospectors.

Some came to know Strauss's jeans as "the two-horse brand" of pants when, in a publicity stunt worthy of a modern-day marketing genius, Strauss reportedly hitched two draft horses to a pair of his denim pants and had them pull in opposite directions. The pants won. In 1886, Strauss added a leather (or oilcloth) patch, featuring a drawing of that advertising event, to the rear of the waistband. The pants became known as 501s about this time; the number supposedly came from a lot number on bolts of denim. In 1890, since the forty-niners were long gone by now, and coins replaced gold dust and nuggets as a medium of trade, Strauss added a fourth pocket, a smaller pocket above the front pocket, designed to hold a watch or a coin.

By the turn of the century, Levi Strauss brought his brothers to San Francisco, and the Levi Strauss Company became even more successful. The pants that built the fortune were still there in the front pages of his 1901 catalog selling for $8.50 a dozen pair, but the humble work clothes that built his fortune had been supplemented by a two-inch cata-

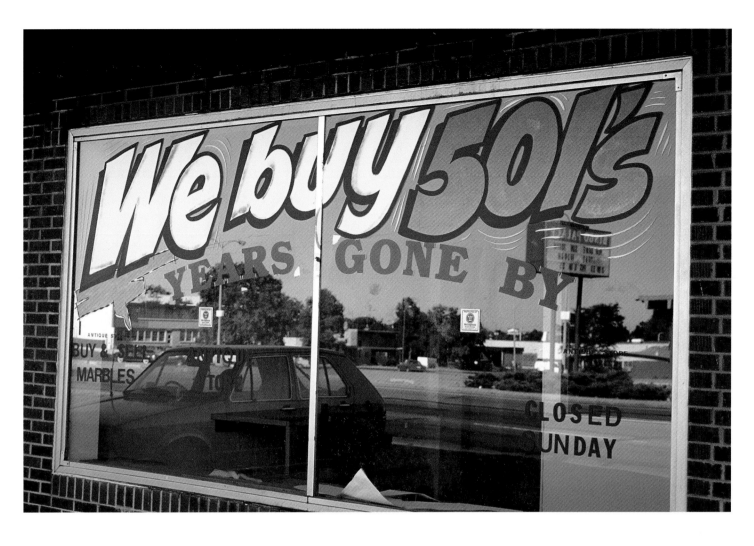

log selling everything from buttons to bows.

Levi Strauss died in 1902, leaving behind millions of dollars, a vastly successful clothing business, and a humble pair of pants that would still bear his name a hundred years after he had sewn his first pair. The 501 jeans have changed little; it was difficult to dabble with perfection. As the city of San Francisco, home of the Levi Strauss Company, had grown almost as fast as the popularity of Levi's pants and had become a cosmopolitan city, a fifth pocket was added to the jeans in 1905, perhaps to carry both wallet and checkbook.

Levi Strauss's jeans clothed the workers who helped to rebuild Levi Strauss and Company following its destruction in the great 1906 earthquake that hit San Francisco. The flames and floods that accompanied the quake weren't enough to destroy the company, and before too long, Levi Strauss and Company was back in business.

In 1922, belt loops were added, eventually replacing suspender buttons on the 501 jeans. The next change wouldn't come until 1936 when the red LEVI'S tab was added to the back pocket. By this time, jeans had become widespread, and the imitators, innovators, and competitors made it necessary for Levi Strauss and Company to further identify its 501 jeans as the original blue jeans. An oilcloth label on a pair of new jeans stated (in part): "This is a pair of Levi's. They are positively superior to any made in the United States and enjoy a national reputation."

Levi's did enjoy a national reputation for many years, being the only blue jeans overall. There just weren't many serious competitors in those early days. It wasn't until 1912 that another major manufacturer came on the blue jeans scene.

THE JEANS THAT BUILT AMERICA

H. D. LEE

In 1849, the same year young Levi Strauss was contemplating going to California, H. D. Lee was born in Vermont. Lee was a hardworking young man and a shrewd investor who eventually parlayed his earnings into a fortune that included oil companies and a wholesale grocery business. From his base in Salina, Kansas, Lee started several large companies that bore his name, but he was not yet known for what was to become the LEE brand of denim clothing. In 1911, Lee found he was having trouble keeping certain goods in stock, especially work-wear items, including overalls and dungarees (made from heavy cotton twill and denim). Seeing a new business opportunity, he made the fateful decision to build his own garment factory in Salina. His first claim to fame in the work-wear business came a few years later when, according to legend, he suggested his firm develop a one-piece, work-wear garment. Apparently, he was responding to a complaint from his chauffeur, who was tired of dirtying his uniform while working on Lee's automobile. The

The H. D. Lee Company had "Something to Crow About" when they competed for their share of the denim work-clothes market with clothing manufactured under the Can't Bust 'Em label, originally a trademark of the Eloesser-Heybemann Company, Inc., of San Francisco that Lee bought in 1946.

legend could be true; the chauffeur inherited $5,000 after Lee's death.

As a result of his chauffeur's complaint, Lee's workers sewed together a jacket and a pair of dungarees, and the Lee Union-All was born. He envisioned this would be the ideal outfit for farm and factory workers wanting to keep their everyday clothes clean while working. The practicality of the new garment changed Lee's fortune forever. The United States Army was so impressed by the Union-All that in 1917, Lee Company was contracted by the army to produce as many pairs as it could, and the Union-All was adopted as the official doughboy fatigue during World War I. By 1917, Lee had introduced more quality and comfort features in overalls, dungarees, and Union-Alls than all its competitors combined. That year, Lee also pioneered the idea of nationally advertising work clothes, and purchased advertisements in *The Saturday Evening Post*.

The predecessor of what would become Lee Riders was introduced in 1924. These were pants made of heavy thirteen-ounce

The Lee leather patch on its denim jeans has become almost as universally recognizable as the Levi's 501s patch.

An early Lee plant facility. Despite many technological advances, denim jeans are still manufactured in much the same way they were decades ago.

denim (Levi's were made of ten-ounce denim at that time), and they were crafted especially for seamen and loggers. The heavy cowboy pants were to follow. By 1926, Lee had initiated a remarkable series of merchandising firsts, including jeans with zippers, more comfortable styling, and tailored sizing.

In 1928, H. D. Lee died of a heart attack in San Antonio, Texas, but like Levi Strauss, he left behind a pair of pants that would bear his name long after his death and a company that would live on to be one of the world's largest denim-clothing manufacturers. Lee's motto, "The Jeans That Built America," is a tribute to his tough, working-man's clothing.

Henry David Lee

The famous Lee brand was designed to actually look like a brand to help enhance the appeal of Lee's cowboy pants.

HOW DEPRESSING
DUST-BOWL DENIM

Out of the ashes of failure, success is often born. The stock market crash of 1929 and the resulting worldwide economic crisis would, ironically, have much to do with the growing success of denim work clothes. The depression hit everyone, but its most visible victim was the manual laborer. The railroad men, the farmers, the factory workers, the carpenters—the working-class men had adopted the bib overall, dungarees, and denim jeans as their uniform. It was this uniform, well suited to the needs of the working man, that became a symbol of America's fighting spirit as the country went to war to combat depression, dust, austerity, and poverty. It was the farmers and factory workers in their working blues who were captured by Work Projects of America (WPA) photographers and who were represented to the country and the world in the pages of *Life*, *Look*, and *The Saturday Evening Post*. Whole families wearing denim, and not much else, were photographed as the stoic foot soldiers in this war on poverty. The

This Oshkosh B'Gosh buckle became commonplace during the depression as hard times necessitated hard-wearing work clothing.

This hard face, captured by photographer Walker Evans during the Great Depression, reflects the raggedness of the people and the clothes that lived through those hard times.

Lee was only one of many
denim manufacturers that
made bib overalls to clothe a
depression-era workforce.

**Denim became the
uniform of the working
class as America
struggled through the
dim days of the
depression. Photograph
by Walker Evans.**

enduring spirit, tenacity, and strength of
these people were mirrored in the simple
strength and dignity of denim. Agonizing
despair could not break the spirit of
Americans, and they fought back towards a
national recovery.

To clothe this army of homeless workers
and hoboes who welcomed some honest work
and a hand up, a multitude of work clothes
manufacturers was born. New brands joined
Lee and Levi during the depression: Blue Bell,
Big Smith, Big Ben, Big Bridge, Buckhide,
Carhart, Union Made, Pay Day, Tuff Nut,
Hercules, and perhaps dozens more. Dustbowl
and depression dreams might not have been
big, but the names of denim clothes were.
Although companies such as Lee saw sales
grow dramatically during these years, the
Great Depression still led to cuts in profits and
wages until the mid-1930s. Out of necessity,
denim may have been the fashion, but it wasn't
fashionable. It was not status wear, fun, or
stylish. It would clothe the human spirit that
had endured those terrible times and emerge
as the look of a new American hero.

The days of America's New Deal further
defined denim. Thousands of workers joined
programs of the National Recovery Act and
wore the red eagle of the NRA on the label of
their overalls and work clothes.

Denim jackets were lined with canteen or

Lee
OVERALLS

blanket material in an attempt to protect workers as they struggled against the cold winds of winter. Jackets became longer in the railroad style, and denim appeared on the backs of prisoners, many of them only victims of the destructive depression days. There was a solidarity among most Americans that had never existed before, a sense of belonging, and of suffering and enduring together. These hardships helped bring about unions, and denim work clothes became a union uniform, often reflected in the names of the garments and the ever-present "Union Made" label.

As the country recovered from the depression, work clothes became something more; they fathered a style and a desire to belong to that working class. Big-city people saw overalls worn by workers in the South and jeans worn by cowboys out West, and they wanted that look. Denim began to stand on its own with the power to transform one's life simply by wearing those magical blue garments. Like some medieval knight's armor, thick, rough denim seemed to suggest protection, offering a feeling of security in very insecure times.

The ancestor of today's Wrangler Company, the Blue Bell Overall Company, had merged with the Big Ben Manufacturing Company in 1926 and emerged from the depression as a major manufacturer of denim

Denim jeans were so tough, many saw double duty as they were handed down from older to younger brother. Photograph by Walker Evans.

Vintage Lee label.

work clothing. The Blue Bell Overall Company changed its name in 1936 to Blue Bell-Globe Manufacturing Company when it bought out Globe Superior Corporation. At that time, these companies were the two largest in the world. Seven years later, the name changed again to a simple Blue Bell, Inc.

Earlier on, the Blue Bell brand stood out for its quality denim railroad wear: clothing tough enough to endure and become some of the first denim collectibles. Before the Europeans and Japanese developed a taste for

Lee introduced its Union-All in 1913. This garment was supposedly invented by Lee's personal chauffeur who inherited $5,000 from Lee for his idea.

the old denim of these American railroad heroes, railroad buffs and collectors in this country were seeking out denim clothing worn by engineers and brakemen during the glory days of railroading in America. Copper, blued steel, and brass buttons with embossed names such as Red Star, Big Ben, Ox Hide, Big Mac, and, of course, Blue Bell adorned the well-worn, faded denims of these railroad workers and were magnets for railroad collectors wanting a precious piece of America's past.

The blue denim overall became the garment of choice for many of America's working class, including railroaders, farmers, mechanics, and others looking for hard-wearing practical work clothes.

T H E   C O U N T R Y
A N D
C O W B O Y   L O O K

DENIM AND DUDES

As important as a toy six-gun, jeans were worn by every youngster who grew up wanting to be a cowboy.

As the country was recovering from its depression days in the late 1930s, Americans began to want new heroes. Radios, magazines, and Saturday matinees brought America a new hero to immortalize, and the new hero wore jeans from the start. On the radio, western swing music had replaced the hillbilly sound of farmers with fiddles in bandannas and bib overalls. The new look was cowboy boots and hats and blue jeans, worn long with rolled-up cuffs to show off colorful inlaid and carved-leather boot tops.

Farm boys and the singing railroad man Jimmie Rodgers were given over to heroes on horseback and singing cowboys such as Gene Autry and Roy Rogers. America went crazy for its cowboys. Lee, Levi Strauss and Company, and a few other brands had already been aligning themselves with the western image and the cowboy. A hair-on-hide leather label on its Lee Rider cowboy

Route 66. As Americans became more mobile and in love with things western, cowboy images pulled travelers off the road to experience another roadside attraction and, perhaps, to buy their first pair of western jeans.

Movie stars such as Gene Autry, Roy Rogers, Hopalong Cassidy, and a dozen others brought the western movie and its cowboy heroes to theaters across the country. They also popularized denim as cowboy pants.

pants and its involvement in the rodeo business made Lee a favorite among many cowboys. Lee Riders were created by Lee in 1924 especially for cowboys, and the seam rivets of earlier pants disappeared in favor of durable, double-strength stitched seams. (Rivets hitting saddles weren't comfortable for cowboys, and they scratched the leather.) In 1936, Lee became the official sponsor of the rodeo circuit, much like today's Wrangler, which sponsors the Professional Rodeo Cowboys Association (PRCA). Everyone knew cowboys were loyal, so Lee figured it was good business to do something for cowboys to assure that loyalty to their brand of cowboy jeans.

Much of Levi Strauss and Company's advertising also catered to this working cowboy market. But it would be America's new-

found prosperity and its love affair with the West and travel that would bring about the greatest growth in this market. Easterners with enough money to vacation were frequently heading west and returning with the cowboy outfits they had purchased while guests at the burgeoning number of guest and dude ranches. The dude ranches of Wyoming, Montana, and Colorado, written up in *Life* magazine travel articles and railroad promotions, guaranteed the city slicker a real taste of the cowboy life. Western style was born. Rodeo cowboys and movie cowboys were a bit more glitzy than real working cowboys, who were mostly living on low wages and in remote solitude, so rodeo cowboys contributed greatly to denim's image as real cowboy clothing. In the style of Buffalo

In 1920, Lee introduced its Buddy Lee doll as a promotional item. The ceramic figures were originally clad in Lee overalls, but their popularity soon led to a larger wardrobe, including railroad uniforms and, of course, cowboy outfits. This doll was one of the first denim-related collectibles and can fetch up to $1,000 in today's market.

The popularity of dude ranches and things western are symbolized in this denim-skirted cowgirl pinup.

Bill and his Wild West Show of the late 1800s, showmen such as Leo Cremer and his tough cowboys in jeans brought the West everywhere with their on-the-road rodeos and cowboy shows.

In the late 1930s, American kids wore toy six-guns low on the hips of their denim dungarees and scuffed up their boots. They wanted to imitate the likes of Gene Autry, Hopalong Cassidy, Roy Rogers, Tom Mix, and others, some of whom were real cowboys before being hogtied by Hollywood fame and becoming kiddie heroes and Saturday matinee idols. But it wasn't long before the denim of the Wild West was being exchanged for military denim.

T H E   B L U E S   F A D E
T O
O L I V E   D R A B

W A R

Were it not for the war, American kids would never have hung up their six-shooters. They would have worn those frayed denim cowboy pants forever. But as their dads picked up war weapons and took off their weekend western-wear jeans to ride off into a different sunset—a world at war—denim cowboy pants began to lose their appeal. But, World War II didn't kill the cowboy craze; it would reappear after the war. Meanwhile, denim went to war, and most of the business that denim manufacturers did at that time was war business. The shortage of Lee garments due to wartime rationing was addressed in a 1943 advertisement in *Life* magazine. Rationing was a way of life, and even though Lee proclaimed itself "In peace or war, the largest selling line of its kind in America," it and most other denim-clothing makers had changed gears to meet the special demands of a wartime economy.

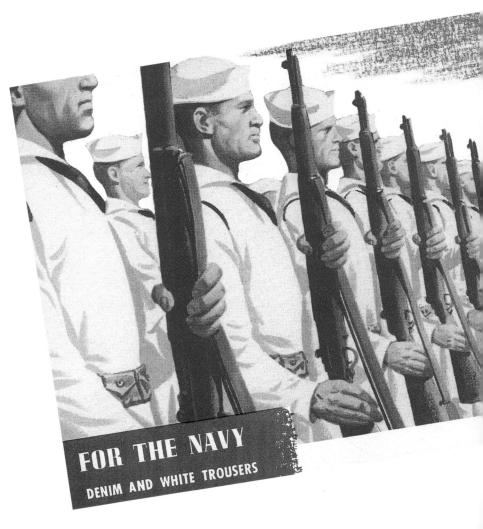

FOR THE NAVY
DENIM AND WHITE TROUSERS

As America went to war, denim manufacturers were enlisted to provide clothing for the armed forces, and their advertising attentions shifted from marketing products to marketing patriotism.

SEWING YOUR WAY TO SUCCESS

IN A WAR JOB WITH A FUTURE!

FOR THE ARMY

◄ KHAKI DRESS PANTS AND SHIRTS

JUNGLE SUITS ►

ALSO:
- All-over one-piece suits
- Denim pants and coats
- Olive drab herringbone jackets and trousers

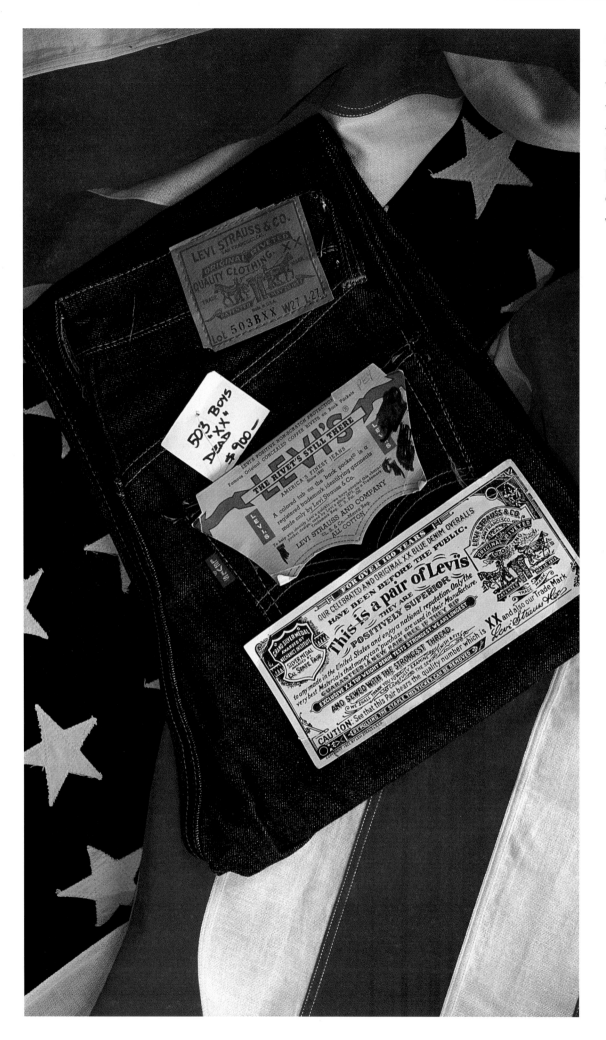

During the denim shortages of the war years, many Americans would have given anything for a new pair of Levi's jeans. Could they have had any idea what collectors fifty years later would be willing to pay?

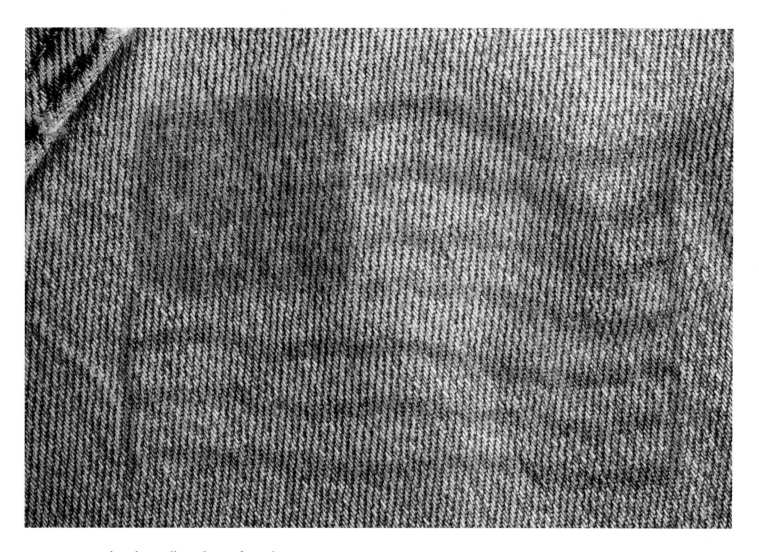

Denim serves as canvas
for a patriotic doodler
who expressed himself
during the war years.

For example, Blue Bell, makers of much of America's work clothing, made the switch from civilian to war production. Company records say more than twenty-four million garments were made by Blue Bell for the armed forces as their requirements skyrocketed. Those garments included jungle suits, denim pants, coats, fatigue pants and jackets, trousers, shirts, and flying suits. Most wartime advertising was directed at patriotism, not at selling products. Product loyalty was maintained by promoting the company's loyalty to the war efforts and America's fighting men. Like most Americans, they hoped the war would soon be over and those fighting men would be needing new pants.

Blue Bell sought workers during wartime as their production switched to making military garments, many of which were made of denim.

AMERICA NEEDS YOU...NOW!

BLUE BELL OFFERS YOU

A WAR JOB

WITH A FUTURE

GET THE FACTS...NO OBLIGATION

Come in to see us today!

T H E   B O O M   B E G I N S

POSTWAR

The shortage of Lee garments due to the wartime material rationing was discussed in a 1943 advertisement in *Life* magazine.

The war would begin to change denim. Sure, the cowboy heroes who rode across the screens on Saturdays before the war would return to battle the bad guys, but now, mostly the bad guys wore the jeans. The good-guy stars were wearing "fancy pants," tailored western pants made by Hollywood tailors such as Manuel and Nudie. The cowboys looked more like western singers than lead slingers—and many of them were. It wasn't enough anymore to be able to ride, rope, shoot, beat the bad guys, and kiss the women. The new western stars had to be able to sing their way into the hearts of the audience. Soon enough, television would keep us home on Saturdays to watch our western heroes.

Denim makers began a renewed attack on the civilian clothing market. The war had taught companies a lot about mass-production methods while making millions of military garments. The companies soon realized that, in the aftermath of the war and with the new American prosperity and abundance, they had better make the switch from making work clothes to making play clothes. One of the biggest markets for this was western wear. The popularity of television and movie westerns was at an all-time high; tourists

Roy Rogers and Dale Evans in a publicity still.

from the East still went west for the dude-ranch experience and came home with their stiff, dark jeans, leather boots, and big hats. But they might make those clothes weekend wear back home. Postwar America wanted to have some fun again, and clothing manufacturers responded. Diversification into western wear led to such changes as the giant company Blue Bell changing its slogan from "The World's Largest Producer of Work Clothes" to "The World's Largest Producer of Work and Play Clothes." This change spawned the birth of the national brand name "Wrangler" in 1947 with a style of jeans made exclusively

for cowboys, and an uninterrupted period of growth began for western jeans.

Today, those same Wrangler jeans are the official jeans of the Professional Rodeo Cowboys Association and are often required wear during rodeo competitions. Rodeo is the one sport in which the spectators can wear the exact same clothes as the athletes, and most do dress western for rodeos. In fact, the "W" design stitched into the two back pockets of Wrangler jeans supposedly stands for "Western Wear." Through allying itself with rodeo stars, Wrangler became almost synonymous with western wear and its cowboy heroes.

DENIM GETS ITS BAD-BOY IMAGE

BLUE JEANS AND BIKERS

Postwar America would soon have a new hero, or in this case, an antihero who wore blue jeans: the biker. Immediately following the war, thousands of service men who had been riding motorcycles in the service and in combat came home with a love for motorcycles (bikes) and the freedom they represented. The bikes most of them had ridden in the war, big Harley-Davidsons, weren't available to the public again until 1947. Many ex-soldiers took to the streets on bikes they had built from parts. They rode old motorcycles and British motorcycles. Many of them radically changed the original design and overall appearance of their motorcycles. These were the first true custom bikes, but not as we know them now. These bikes, with their stripped-down look, were known as "bobbers" or "choppers" for their bobbed fenders or cut-up and modified frames.

As many ex-soldiers joined together or with buddies back home to

Fiercely proud of their individuality, bikers nevertheless embraced a common way of dress, and that uniform demanded denim.

share in their love of motorcycles and the freedom of the open road, motorcycle clubs began to spring up around the country. A certain segment of these riders began to exhibit what were once called unpopular riding practices, such as using unmuffled exhaust pipes, weaving in and out of traffic, using excessive speed, and generally "cutting up" at rallies and race meets. A few of these groups, most notably in California where many veterans relocated following the war, were almost warlike in their aggression and customs.

A classic Harley-Davidson motorcycle hangs like an angel over stacks of used Levi's jeans in a clothing store in Chicago.

Unleashed on civilian roads, some of these disaffected veterans became known as "outlaw bikers." Unfortunately, the press and notoriety they were receiving colored just about anyone who rode a motorcycle. The image of motorcycles and those who rode them would forever change following one of the most notorious events in postwar motorcycle history. What made the rowdy antics of a bunch of beer-guzzling, bobber-riding, outlaw motorcyclists in 1947 Hollister, California, so interesting and caused such great alarm across America was the *Life* magazine photographers who were there to capture it all. Perhaps these "bikers," as they were beginning to be called, did act up for the cameras; perhaps some of the pictures were even staged; but somehow, this out-of-proportion publicity became the basis for the Marlon Brando movie *The Wild One*.

American classics.
Vintage motorcycles
and vintage jeans just
get better with age.

PAINTED BY
REX PEACOCK

Marlon Brando glamorized the rebel look of blue jeans in the classic 1953 motorcycle gang movie *The Wild One*.

Loosely based on the event in Hollister as depicted by the national media, *The Wild One* was released July 4, 1953, and signaled the birth of the biker cult. This Stanley Kramer movie became the blueprint for every other grade B, outlaw-gang/wild-biker movie to be made, a genre that lasted for decades. Although Marlon Brando actually rode a Triumph in that movie, it was Harley-Davidson that suffered over the "outcry from this aberrant and abhorrent behavior of this undesirable element" of motorcycle riders.

While it can't necessarily be proven that *The Wild One* actually spawned any motorcycle gangs of wild bikers, Marlon Brando and Lee Marvin did give national exposure to the biker look, a look Marlon Brando first made famous in the movie *A Streetcar Named Desire*. It's not just a look for outlaw bike gangs, but a look coveted and imitated by a generation of teenage rebels—what today would be called "biker wannabes." A person didn't have to ride a motorcycle then or now to dress the part. All it required was a black leather motorcycle jacket, a T-shirt, black leather engineer boots with a buckled strap across the ankle, and of course, a pair of jeans. Almost exclusively, these jeans were Levi's button-fly 501s. The essential element of the biker look called for the jeans to be rolled up at the cuff, well-worn, if not greasy, thumbs insolently hooked in the front pockets. A scowling, sideways sneer and long sideburns completed the look. Bad boys had ridden their way into the American culture and they, and the look, were here to stay.

Denim adorned with pins, buttons, badges, and patches is biker wear as personal as a tattoo.

CLASSIC DENIM DAYS

THE FIFTIES

Marlon Brando, Elvis Presley, and James Dean helped to bring the bad-boy image to mainstream America. A whole new sound, rock 'n' roll, emerged as the soundtrack for a generation that rapidly rejected the styles and values of its parents. Tired of the drab sameness of a world in war uniforms, rebels and rockers slipped into tight denim jeans to proclaim their individuality and to flaunt their youth. Jeans became the uniform of the young. Millions of teenagers joined those rebels and rockers in expressing their individuality and uniqueness by dressing almost identically—at least, as far as wearing denim jeans. The uniform of nonconformity had arrived. From that point on, jeans would be forever linked with youth and serve as an expression of youth, no matter how old the wearers grew. Aging Americans may not be able to dance all night, feel the pain and passion of teenage love, and dream teen dreams, but they will always have jeans as a symbol of the fountain of youth.

In prewar and pre-rock 'n' roll America, denim was strictly utilitarian. There was no style or status associated with a pair of denim pants or a jacket. Perhaps denim suggested lower class, poverty, or manual laborer. What

James Dean in jeans became a national symbol for rebellious youth in the 1950s movie classic *Giant.*

The popularity of James Dean and denim came together in jeans sold as "In the Style of James Dean's pants." This vintage collectible rests on an early Porsche like the one Dean died in back in 1955. He, no doubt, died with his jeans on.

THE JEAN

J.S.D

IN THE STYLE OF JAMES DEAN'S PANTS

Warner Bros' Pictures
without a cause
East of Eden
GIANT

glory it did have probably came from cow-boys—strong, free-riding, masculine loners who lived mostly by their own rules. That image simply transferred to the lone-wolf motorcycle riders of the fifties who, to many, were mechanized cowboys and the rightful heirs to the title of American loner. Jeans, like rock 'n' roll, became subversive, and when Elvis Presley swayed his hips sugges-tively in his jeans, denim became sexual. No adult, unless he was a farmer or a rancher, was going to be wearing denim. First, it was too low class and reminiscent of the depres-sion, and later, it was too vulgar and too young.

Jeans and denim clothing took on a new identity. They were no longer work clothes; they were play clothes. The casual look was born, and jeans came to represent a new-found American ideal—leisure time. Elvis and James Dean wore the uniform like gener-als in a war against the old morality. *Rebel Without a Cause* became an icon for a new

youthful culture, and it taught us how to dress. T-shirts and jeans, Brando's signature wardrobe, bespoke a new set of values. Jeans symbolized SEX.

Marilyn Monroe never looked like a farmer in her jeans. Denim pants began to encase young sexual energy, and the fashion industry responded with jeans being worn lower on the hips and tighter. Just as the gold miners in the days of Levi Strauss had jumped into a horse trough to get their Levi's to fit a bit better, teenagers were now wearing stiff, dark blue, Levi's 501 shrink-to-fits into the family bathtub. "Guaranteed to shrink" became an advertising label that parents would never understand. Jeans were guaran-teed to shrink to fit and to "fade out to the sky" that deep indigo color. They were worn tight as a second skin. They had to be turned inside out to get them off. Putting them on was a ritual and sometimes a group effort, as teens wiggled and pulled denim an inch at a time, sucking in their waists and holding

Clark Gable and Marilyn Monroe gave denim a national audience with their wardrobes for the movie *The Misfits*. It appears Marilyn's jeans didn't misfit her.

Newsweek

MARCH 21, 1966   40¢

The Teen-Agers

A Newsweek Survey of What They're Really Like

After publicity shots such as this were seen across the country, Marilyn Monroe helped to popularize the look of denim. Cowboy clothing, once work wear, now became sexy.

Teens took to denim as a badge of rebellion in the fifties, and a decade later it was still sending the same message.

their breaths to get that zipper closed or last button buttoned. "Tight Fittin' Jeans" became more than a song; they were an erotic signal recognized the world over. Sexier than no clothes at all, jeans began to suggest good times to a whole generation.

The good times rolled—rock 'n' rolled—throughout the fifties for denim. Manufacturers responded to the new demand for denim with a variety of different products. Seeing they were about to lose the adult market, jeans makers came out with dress jeans in whites and colors, including center creases and pleats, with narrower legs and "new" sanforized fabrics. For the kids, they introduced novelty jeans embellished with cute paintings or armored with decorative studs

114

"Dusty" (Roy Rogers Jr.) and his brother "Sandy" (Harry John David Rogers), sons of western movie star Roy Rogers, show why kids soon crawled holes in their jeans.

and rhinestones. A new children's product, Double-knees by Lee, came out in 1957 as an answer to moms' complaints about their kids going through the knees of their jeans in a crawling hurry. Other manufacturers almost went broke promising a new replacement pair of jeans if children wore out the knees. It was almost instant reincarnation for dead or dying kids' jeans. As jeans moved from function to fashion, whole families were again wearing denim clothing.

Jeans became as American as Coca-Cola when dozens of new manufacturers jumped on the denim days of glory. A world partly recovered from a devastating decade of war wanted the good life and the American dream. There began to be an overseas

demand for denim jeans. In response to this worldwide desire, Lee opened its first International Division in 1959 and its first overseas plant in 1963. In 1964, Lee was awarded a presidential award for making an outstanding contribution to the export expansion of the United States. Imitators and designers all over Europe came out with their own brands of jeans, but somehow they lacked denim credibility. The young people creating this demand wanted the real thing, and they weren't settling for cheap copies or local brands. A very early black market in American denim (most notably, Levi's button-fly 501s) had begun as the world entered the turbulent decade of the sixties.

What are a couple of movie stars doing in jeans? Making a movie called "Bikini Beach." Why did they pick jeans by Wrangler? For the same reasons you will—as soon as you try them on.

Because Wrangler makes jeans that move like part of you. Because you can have them trim and slim as you like: they're Sanforized.® Because they come in a whole kit and kaboodle of styles and colors—for guys and girls both. Because Wrangler is tough and can really take it, no matter how active you are!

Go see the movie. Wear your Wrangler jeans when you do.

Annette Funicello and Frankie Avalon in the Wrangler jeans they wear in the American International Pictures Pathecolor and Panavision production, "Bikini Beach." Wrangler for guys: jeans, stretch jeans and regular, walking shorts, western shirts and socks. Wrangler for girls: jamaicas, knee pants, jeans, stretch and regular, in a range of colors, with coordinated shirts. For guys and girls: Wrangler western jackets. Wrangler is a division of Blue Bell, Inc., 350 Fifth Ave., New York, N.Y. 10001.

Annette FUNICELLO **&** **Frankie** AVALON **in Wrangler® Jeans**

The appearance of young American teen idols and movie stars in magazines and advertisements helped lead a dramatic growth in the popularity of denim clothing. Such stars as Annette Funicello and Frankie Avalon helped make denim mainstream clothing for teens.

DENIM HITS THE STREET
THE SIXTIES

In the early 1960s, jeans had just about become accepted wear to the parents and school principals of kids who first wore them as a deliberate defiance of the social norm. Fashion adopted denim and began to mold it into something more socially acceptable. Softer, brushed denim was invented before stonewashed or acid-washed denim. There was colored denim; no-iron or permanent-press denim; lightweight denim; stretch denim for our postwar, prosperous, bigger bodies; and denim degraded as it was mixed with other fabrics. A generation had thrown stiff, dark denim in the faces of its elders, and the elders gave it back to them sanforized. All the fight had been taken out of it. The James Dean estate was marketing his own brand of jeans. It had become middle class, softened (literally and figuratively), and as threatening as blue-suede shoes. Even rock 'n' roll, it seemed, had abandoned denim. The British rock-group invasion was beginning. The Beatles didn't wear jeans. British rockers weren't raw and tough like real

American standards, including Levi's jeans and Elvis, suffered in popularity in the wake of the British invasion of rock groups such as the Beatles in the early sixties.

American rockers; they were cute—even their name seemed to suggest cuteness. British groups wore suits or psyche-delic, Edwardian-inspired clothes from Carnaby Street. If they did wear denim, rock groups were seen and named differently. The Animals wore jeans, didn't they? But Carnaby Street was just a fad. Denim was a style—an American classic—and most Americans still wore them and felt more comfortable than they ever did in wide-wale corduroys or striped, bell-bottomed trousers.

Jeans makers such as Lee switched from keeping up with the demands of postwar prosperity, to staying on top of the quickening rhythm of fashion change. The postwar baby boom had spawned an explosion in the number of teens who, according to Lee, "by 1965 would spend $3.5 billion on apparel, much of it on jeans and other casual attire." Despite the American love affair with jeans, polyester and permanent-press fabrics began to have a dramatic impact on the jeans market, as America looked for an easier way and more leisure time.

The popularity of such American idols as James Dean, killed in a car crash in the fifties, seemed to grow to legendary status in the sixties. The denim-clad image of Dean helped keep denim in the sixties fashion forefront.

That leisure time was often spent in front of America's millions of television sets, and for the first time ever, those televisions were bringing images of war, death, destruction, poverty, world chaos, and the Cold War threat of nuclear annihilation into cozy little family rooms. Suddenly, a pacified youth began to act up again. The millions of postwar children, the baby boomers, had become a force to be reckoned with, not only in the marketplace as consumers but also in America's political arenas. The first generation that had grown up living the American dream turned their backs

Mass-produced "novelty jeans" from the fifties such as these gave way to denim as self-expression, when American teens began to customize and decorate their own jeans in the sixties.

on the providers of that good life, seeing the providers as shallow hypocrites and rejecting their values and morals. They also rejected their clothing. Young people didn't want pre-pressed and polyester; they wanted authentic, natural, and functional. They wanted their own style, but they also wanted to go back to America's roots. Denim jeans and shirts were the perfect uniform for this disenfranchised army of teenagers and young people. They grew their hair long. More women began to wear pants and were no longer seen as tomboys when they did. The young women hitchhiked and marched alongside the young men as they traveled across the country, protesting war, nuclear arms, and aggression. Denim became a canvas as "flower power" became the rallying cry for these youths. They painted themselves and their clothing with flowers, peace signs, and slogans. Jeans became a badge of recognition again, uniting those who wore them in common causes and signaling allegiance to antiwar and antiestab-lishment "brothers and sisters" out in the streets who fought for civil rights.

Denim became as free and colorful as the idealistic hippies who wore it during those "summers of love" in the middle and late sixties. It was a time to get loose and loosen up the uptight morals of authority, or the establishment. Clothing became looser to reflect that, especially jeans. The tapered and pegged skintight jeans of the late fifties and early sixties were out of style. Flower children "kicked out the jams," ripped out

the seams. Big, bright, colorful, flowered, and paisley inserts were added when jeans seams were torn open to make pants loose and wide at the bottom. Bell-bottom jeans were part of the new uniform, but not those mass-produced bell-bottoms and other denim pretenders. They had to be real, and they had to be personal. Personalized by the addition of bells, paintings, fabric inserts, or fringe, denim became an art form, and it became the item of street fashion. It was actually antifashion as young people sought to revolutionize everything from their gov-ernment, to their sexual and moral values, to their music, food, and religion. It was a great time of change for most things, but the old original Levi's 501s, unchanged in almost 100 years, were still the jeans of choice for these hippies, flower children, and revolutionists.

Half a million peace- and music-loving young people went to Woodstock wearing jeans, if they wore anything for very long, in that summer of free love and "letting it all hang out." Inhibitions were something for squares and straights. By 1969, denim enjoyed a new status as revolutionary wear. Coupled with cast-off army jackets and com-bat or hiking boots, jeans said something about a person's beliefs, desires, sexuality, politics—all without speaking a word. Jeans were the secret signal among the freedom fighters in the American streets. They explained a person's status but were not a status symbol. At least, not in the sixties.

DENIM DOES DISCO
THE SEVENTIES

For many, even those still wearing denim, the seventies were an embarrassment. The revolutionary and radical sixties gave way to the shallow glitz and glamour of the seventies. Rock disappeared. Disco appeared. The sexual revolution gave birth to the self-revolution, and Americans were no longer into causes but into themselves. Money, fame, and fortune were the new ideals, and jeans had to mirror those ideals. Most wouldn't chose to go back to the seventies, nor would they choose to wear the clothing worn while seeking out the spotlight. This was the era of the leisure suit, what jeans maker Lee called "a sporty interpretation of the business suit." Introduced by Lee in 1972, it was wildly successful and popular with adults who, according to Lee, ". . . began to share in the style revolution previously dominated by the younger generation." Some style revolution.

Big collars, big—no, HUGE—bell-bottoms, colors not found in nature, slick fabrics, even Elvis shed his jeans for his own interpretation of the leisure suit. Some fans missed the old Elvis and wondered if he still might wear jeans at home in Graceland. Rockers became superstars and began to look like carnival acts. Circuslike in their use of

glittery makeup and elaborate costumes once worn only by trapeze artists, it was no longer enough just to play and sing rock music; it had to be performed. Performers replaced singers. Designer denim replaced jeans.

Denim started to speak different languages. In the sixties, it had united a generation and emphasized the togetherness of thoughts and philosophies; in the seventies, denim became status wear. It led to separateness. The kind of denim chosen for wear defined the wearer. Different brands allied themselves with different groups of people. Whether a person wore Lees, Wranglers, or Levi's had a lot to do with how she was accepted by society—to say nothing of designer jeans. Haight-Ashbury hippies were no longer counterculture, and tour busses with tourists from the Midwest drove those streets fruitlessly looking for a flower child. Designer jeans were at the forefront of this change in denim. In the seventies, Americans quit having garden-variety lives and began having "lifestyles." Jeans were available for every lifestyle. Rocker, rebel, redneck, Rotarian, it didn't matter—jeans were styled to suit any taste.

Fashion designers neutered denim, creating unisex jeans. However, the designers'

Jane Fonda and Robert Redford in the movie *The Electric Horseman* carry on the tradition of stars in denim set by Marilyn Monroe and Clark Gable in the fifties.

statement or soaking in a hot tub with new jeans. This was mass-produced custom and the beginning of instant gratification for jeans wearers.

But overseas, where much of the world was in love with America while Americans were only in love with themselves, there was still a great appreciation for things American, especially for American things from the fifties. From James Dean, Marilyn Monroe, Marlon Brando, Harley-Davidson motor-cycles, old biker jackets, ducktail hairdos, Chevrolets, cowboys, and the Marlboro Man, to reruns of old American television pro-grams and movies, old American classics and heroes took on revered icon status across England and most of Europe. Jeans, most notably Levi's 501s, began to take on leg-endary status, and a strong secondary market in used American blue jeans began to develop. No one really understands why. Could it be in a world jealous of America culture that the next best thing to being American is looking American? Or, do non-Americans just recognize classic quality with thousands of years of culture behind them, while Americans seem to have appreciation for only the moment?

Andy Warhol, pop-art master and one of the voices of the 1970s, predicted the short-lived "fame for fifteen minutes" glory given to any American pop idol or icon. He also put a zippered crotch shot of jeans on a Rolling Stone album cover, *Sticky Fingers*, in 1971. At that time, Mick Jagger, lead singer for the Rolling Stones, was wearing skintight lycra jumpsuits, a stripped-down version of Elvis's regalia. Flea markets in London, Paris, and Berlin were stacked high with cast-off, well-worn American Levi's. In 1971, a Levi's 501 advertisement in a London theater had cow-boys and real jeans. A pair of Levi's 501s on the black market in Russia could be worth hundreds of dollars. The rest of the world

Denim still served as a young person's security blanket and defied disco polyester clothing's popularity as the wardrobe of the seventies.

attempts to make statements with all the dif-ferent looks of denim backfired; denim no longer said much. It became too diluted. Once jeans implied a certain attitude and way of living; then, they began to imply how much money their wearers would spend on a pair of jeans. Price seemed no object. In 1979, designer jeans were a billion-dollar business. Designed mostly for women, jeans came lace-trimmed, painted, studded, embroidered, colored, cut, prewashed, and preshrunk. No more making a wearable art

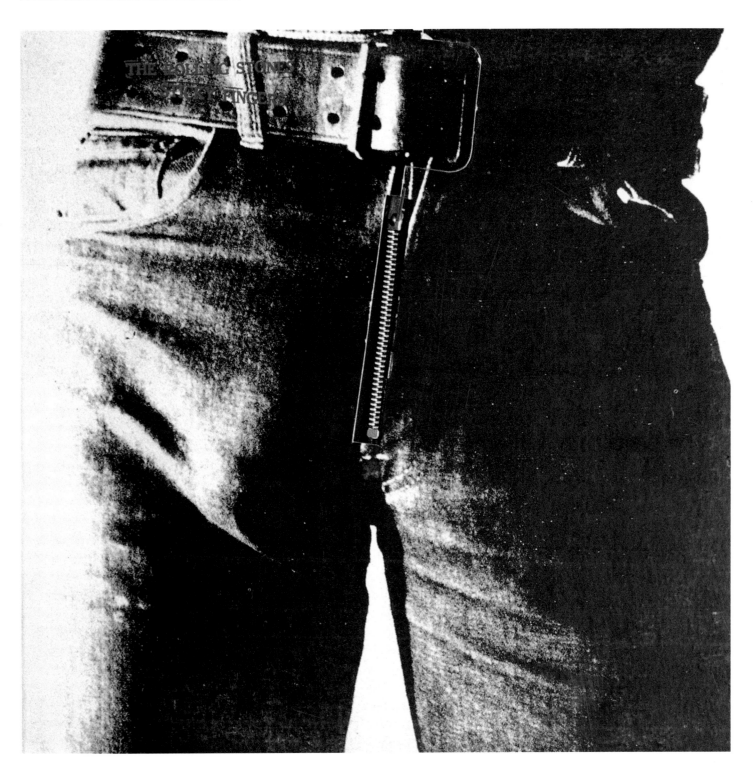

could still see what Americans had lost track of—the simple, comfortable, denim jeans that said "American classic."

It seemed the only Americans wearing real jeans were cowboys, construction workers, and those who were too poor or unsophisticated to live in a condo, snort cocaine, and really be "into" style. The Village People dressed like hard hats, cowpokes, and gay bikers and didn't wear designer jeans. Denim became one of the complex signals for gays

before they came out of the closet. Still, the majority of Americans wore only designer denim, and the jeans manufacturers attempted to give Americans what they wanted.

As a result, Levi Strauss and Company had lost touch with its roots. Diversification into fashion clothing and their own retail stores had them turning their backs on the product that made them famous. There was talk of discontinuing the 501 jeans—just

Andy Warhol, grand master of pop art, created this cover for the Rolling Stones' 1970s album *Sticky Fingers*, which featured a working zipper on printed denim jeans.

needed to think of themselves as more worldly and cosmopolitan. The Euro-American look began, and jeans with French and Italian names, though usually made in Hong Kong, were being sold to them. To make the jeans appear even more sophisticated and worldly, they were expensive. But even at a hundred dollars a pair, disco-designer denim sold. It sold so well that advertising denim jeans would change forever. Sex, or the hint of sex, would sell us our jeans. Sex sold so well, in fact, that for the first time in marketing history, it was no longer even necessary to show the product. Jeans advertisements sometimes had no jeans in them; Americans were being sold an idea, an emotion, a feeling, a promise of hot sex, not of warm denim. As the era of free love was replaced by the sexual revolution, the soldier of sex would again declare denim the uniform of the day.

Americans were too sophisticated to see anything from the fifties as stylish. They wanted newness, and styles kept changing to please them. They already were making fun of their sixties bell-bottoms, feeling smugly hip in their seventies flared legs.

In the United States, good ol' American jeans were almost dead—the death certificate signed in 1978 by Gloria Vanderbilt, Calvin Klein, Ralph Lauren, and dozens of other designers who pitched their jeans with varying levels of snob appeal. Seventies fern bars and discos had bouncers to check patrons for the "right kind" of jeans before they were allowed in their clubs. America began to wear denim to work, but it wasn't work clothing anymore. Denim was worn with tweed jackets, cashmere sweaters, and diamonds. In this decade of conspicuous consumption, the name of the maker of the jeans became more important then the jeans themselves, and as the seventies wound down, designers were glorified as denim demigods.

talk. The company's image had been built on working men's clothing, tough and durable and built to last. Fashion was too fleeting, too fickle to change something that had worked for more than a hundred years.

Denim designers, and there were many as designer jeans began to take over the market, turned their backs on American classicism and any links with the fifties. Americans

THEY SHOOT DENIM DON'T THEY

THE EIGHTIES

The kiss of denim on the fifteen-year-old body of Brooke Shields welcomed jeans into the eighties. In a sly reference to not wearing any underwear, Brooke told us, "Nothing Comes Between Me and My Calvins." Calvin Klein sold millions of jeans. Women's groups pointed accusing fingers and claimed Klein was peddling kiddie-porn instead of pants. Designer jeans lived to see another decade. Because jeans customers claimed they wanted more individuality in their clothing, Levi Strauss and Company cut back denim production on its 501s and regular jeans. Also, jeans were too tight for the fitness-conscious consumer of the eighties. The gluttony, selfishness, indulgence, and overindulgence of the seventies was dead. Americans were finally, though gradually, becoming aware of their excesses, and they had an almost fanatical drive to clean up, slim down, and simplify their lives, especially towards the end of the eighties. Promises were made. Drugs and booze were out; health was in. Cheap, instant gratification was out; saving the world was in. The young joined the ex-hippies in the eighties

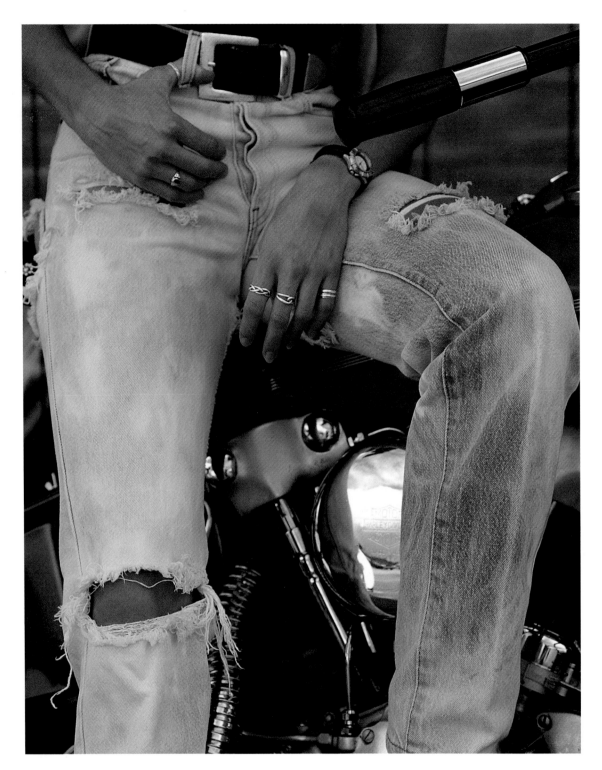

The look of the eighties: a perfectly restored vintage Harley-Davidson and a perfectly worn and torn pair of jeans.

version of revolution. It was time to tear down the old and rip out those greedy, money-worshiping, self-indulgent days of the seventies, starting with jeans.

It might have begun with the punk movement in Europe. It might have been a display of disdain for anything flaunting wealth. It could have been simply a fad, another wave in the ebb and flow of denim custom. Somebody, somewhere, sometime, slashed his jeans. Or, maybe he just tore

them a little bit. Then a little bit more. Then things got out of hand. People spilled bleach on their jeans—their new jeans. They roughed them up. They ripped them. Quick-thinking American entrepreneurs who sensed a trend, blew holes in jeans with double-barreled shotguns and attached the spent shell as proof that the jeans really had been shot. Blown away—all in the name of fashion.

Americans, it seemed, were tired of the

Somehow each "new look" of a generation incorporates denim into the latest style taking off.

In the footsteps of James Dean,
American stars such as Bruce
Springsteen proclaim denim as *Born
in the USA* to a new generation.

BORN IN THE U.S.A./BRUCE SPRINGSTEEN

perhaps in more of a hurry than ever before to enjoy their relaxation. Despite their displeasure with the instant gratification of the past, they wanted the new good life, and they wanted it now. Jeans makers were happy to oblige. Just as in the fifties when they gave us time-saving permanent press, no-iron denim fabrics, now they would be happy to supply—for a price—something that we used to have to wait for: worn-out, or more correctly, worn-in jeans. Pioneered by Maritime Bachellerie and François Girbaud in 1965, the concept of selling worn jeans was not a new one. These French designers decided denim was too stiff and went about developing a process to soften and fade new denim. First, they would wash each pair four or five times, then scrape the fabric with sandpaper. This eventually spawned the stonewashing process whereby jeans were washed with pumice stones to soften the garments and give them a well-worn appearance. Bachellerie and Girbaud would go on to father other technological advances in jeans, including baggy jeans, the concept of "slouchy street chic," and, their company claims, torn and destroyed jeans.

designer-inspired trendiness that had permeated almost all of fashion. It had become a cliche, and the eighties generation hated cliches. But the designers hated losing money more, so they wised up and soon had Americans paying more money for ripped and torn, half-destroyed jeans than they had paid for perfectly good ones. Things were going full circle in a hurry. In a response to this more comfort-seeking, healthful-minded America, jeans manufacturers worked overtime to deliver. Though Americans wanted to consider themselves laid back, they were

Designer jeans sales had peaked in 1981 and were heading downhill. Consumers didn't want or need another designer label of jeans. They wanted their old jeans back but with a lot of life still in them if possible.

The problem with jeans was that they had such a short "perfect" life—the wonderful time when they were just the right softness

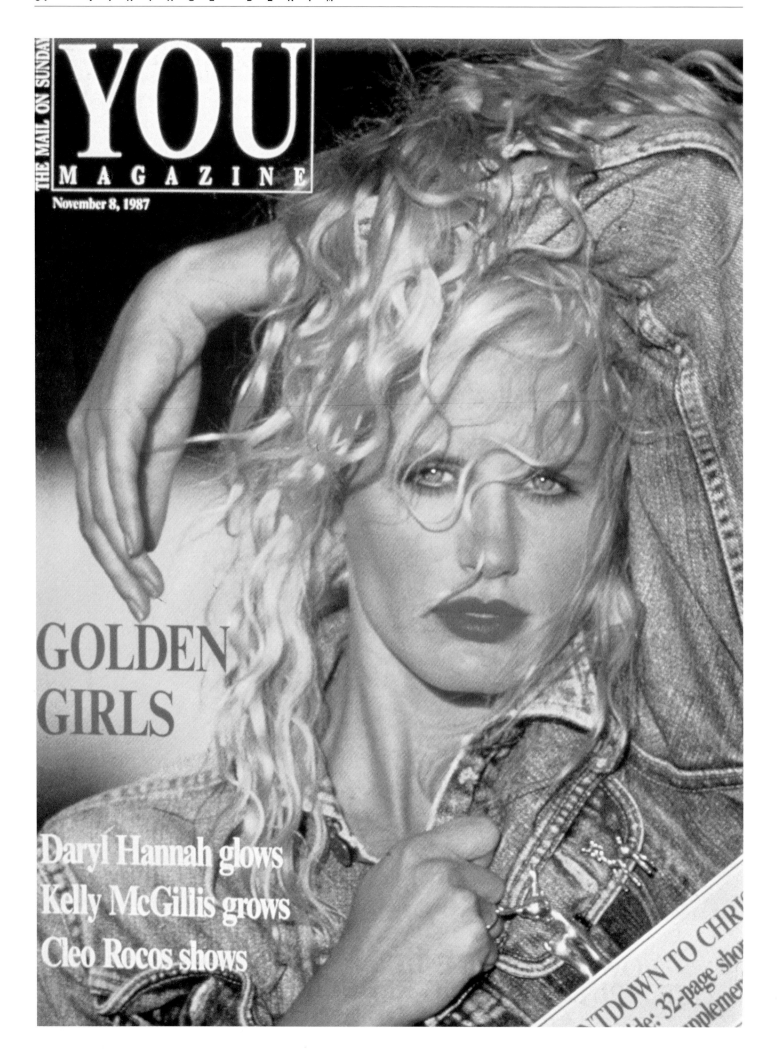

THE MAIL ON SUNDAY

YOU
MAGAZINE

November 8, 1987

GOLDEN GIRLS

Daryl Hannah glows
Kelly McGillis grows
Cleo Rocos shows

...TDOWN TO CHRI...
32-page sho...
...upplemen...

and color of faded blue—what 1970s singer/songwriter Cat Stevens called "faded out to the sky." This usually took a few years and a few dozen trips through the washer and dryer. Just when they became perfect, the fabric was usually so thin that holes would appear, and jeans would go from being perfect to being worn out and ready for the rag bag. This time, the time right before jeans were worn out, was special and wonderful because the wearer had earned those perfect jeans.

Manufacturers such as Lee and Levi Strauss and Company knew about this. Realizing that customers became more attached to their jeans as they became more faded and worn, they began toying with washing their new jeans in chemicals such as bleach and softeners, coining the term "acid-washed." This terminology was a misnomer for most companies, because they didn't actually use acids. But they did try about everything else. Lee said they ultimately experimented with hundreds of objects to prematurely age their jeans, including "shredded car tires, bottle caps, golf balls, rope and wood." But no single item worked as well as pumice, a rock formed by volcanic action and used to soften hands and feet and eliminate calluses. So, between the stones and the chemicals, worn-out new jeans could now be bought, and the age of stonewashing was still with us. Lee claimed they spent more than $2 million a year on rocks from around the world to stonewash their jeans. Because of the battering jeans take during the process, much tougher and more (about twelve times

more) expensive thread had to be used. So, worn-out pants were sold for more than regular jeans, and manufacturers could barely keep up with the demand.

Still, stonewashing and acid-bleaching weren't for denim purists. Customers who took new, dark blue pairs of jeans to the check-out counter got funny looks from store clerks, who knew the jeans wouldn't be wearable until they had seen at least three trips through the wash, so why not just buy the ones already broken in? Even so, some buyers were returning to the standard quality of years past, and original Levi's 501s were selling well again. Coca-Cola had learned the lesson when it brought out new Coke; the lesson was that people wanted "the real thing," the thing they were used to.

Some very minor changes took place across the world of denim in the 1980s. New, faster, and cheaper methods of putting together pants were being employed by manufacturers. This meant less waste of material and less time and expense to make them, but in some cases this also meant that the end result was poor quality. Some changes were insignificant to the manufacturer, but to the jeans purist, the connoisseur, any change mattered.

The red thread that ran down the inside of the leg seam on either side of a pair of Levi's 501s disappeared in 1985. The size of looms changed, and the red line that marked the edge of the woven fabric was gone. No one would notice or care, would they? But just as small changes made in the 501 jeans over the past 100 years could be traced and used as a kind of "carbon dating" to determine when a 501 was made, so could this minor change date the older Levi's. This minor change, which would mean nothing to Levi's or most 501 buyers at the store, would mean a lot—and a lot of money to a growing breed of denim devotee: the Collector.

Movie star Daryl Hannah strikes a "Mona Levi's" pose in a faded denim jacket.

BIG YEN FOR OLD DENIM
DEALERS AND COLLECTORS

Prior to 1980, most worn-out American blue jeans became painting cloths, went to the Salvation Army or Goodwill, were made into rags, or were simply thrown out. True enough, a minuscule amount of used jeans, primarily Levi's 501s, were finding their way overseas and being sold at flea markets and secondhand shops and stalls. Despite the rumors and urban legends that told of a pair of jeans selling for $1,000 in Russia, many people weren't getting wealthy selling the discarded denim of America. Old jeans were street fashion or were for cultists in love with things American. Germany, France, and England seemed to provide the biggest demand for used blues. If a person wanted a pair of secondhand jeans in this country, almost any thrift store could oblige him for a buck a pair. And a lot of those were good jeans— almost new, sometimes, because American denim was so tough that many people outgrew their jeans before they wore them out.

As rare as cheap gas, vintage denim is being sought on back roads and in small towns of America.
Right: Secondhand and vintage denim have become big business.

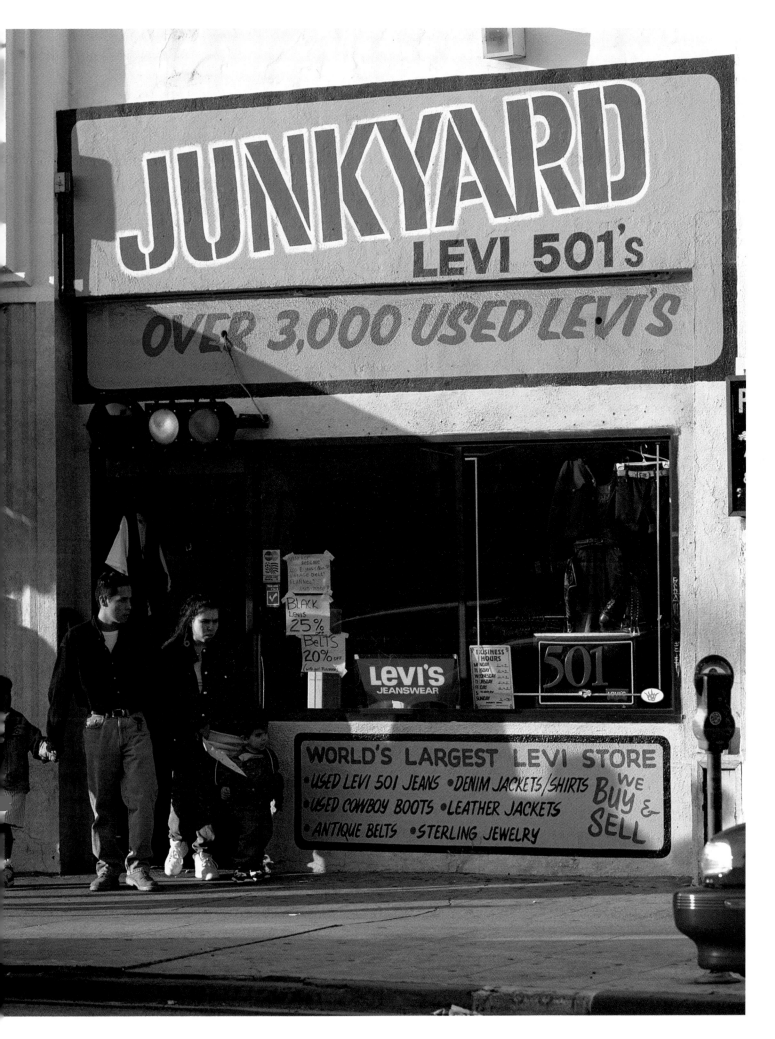

Like the proverbial pot of gold at the end of the rainbow, many lucky vintage hunters have found valuable denim treasure in very unlikely places.

In addition to that, with the ever-changing fickle buying habits of many Americans, there was a lot of denim out there that never sold while the next "hot" thing went on display. Often, it would get stored away or simply buried in a basement for decades. These items were known in the trade as "dead stock," which inventory shop owners had but couldn't sell for one reason or another. It seemed even the most diligent of merchants would always end up with some dead stock to dispose of, and it if didn't get thrown out, it was stashed in stockrooms or basements— anywhere as long as it was out of the way. As the popularity of wearing and collecting vintage clothing grew in this country (some say

Denim dealers and collectors know their details. A sampling of vintage buttons used on early Blue Bell garments.

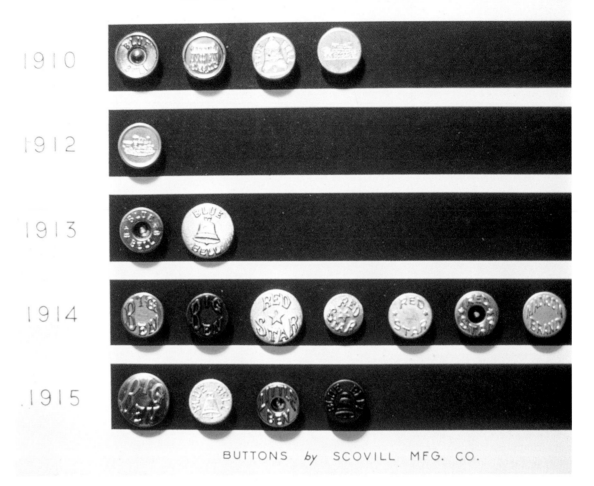

BLUE BELL INC.

1910

1912

1913

1914

1915

BUTTONS *by* SCOVILL MFG. CO.

it was a phenomenon that emerged in the antimaterialistic days of the hippies in the sixties), much of that new but old stock, or dead stock, began to see the light of day again. There were shops in Hollywood along Melrose Avenue that were completely stocked with this old merchandise—some of it more than forty years old—but still with the original labels and, occasionally, the original price tags attached. And it wasn't an item or two. Often there were racks of the same jacket, in all sizes, in all colors—the height of fashion from 1937—all in almost as good condition as when the original merchandise left the factory.

The majority of the dead stock was denim. Except for its novelty value, it wasn't worth much in those days, at least not to most Americans who would rather just buy a brand new pair of jeans. But there were some

who looked at those old dusty piles of blue and saw green. Just as with any other new product, all a merchant had to do was fill a demand. If no demand existed, they simply created one.

It is unclear which American entrepreneurs created the demand; many claim credit. But a few young Japanese who were in tune to their peers in Japan and their desire for things old and American, were busy in those early days of the decade rounding up the bits and pieces of American culture and sending them back to Japan. A demand was created for old American blue jeans.

Was it truly a fad, or was it a plan carefully contrived by the few who had the supply? And shrewdly, the supply was leaked out into the marketplace ever so slowly. With Americans going through millions of pairs of denims a year, to say nothing of what

Vintage Lee advertising.

Lee TAILORED SIZES

TALL—LARGE   AVERAGE   TALL—STOUT   SHORT—STOUT   TALL—SLIM   SHORT—SLIM

- Lee *"Tailored Sizes"* are produced only by The H. D. Lee Company.
- Lee *"Tailored Sizes"* are designed to correctly fit men of all heights and build.
- Lee *"Tailored Sizes"* eliminate strain, prolonging the life of the garment and giving the wearer more working freedom and comfort.

- Lee *"Tailored Sizes"* are styled to give the best possible appearance and fit.
- Lee *"Tailored Sizes"* are preferred by men who live in work clothes all day long.
- Lee *"Tailored Sizes"* are made of exclusive LEE fabrics, woven and dyed to LEE specifications assuring complete satisfaction and the utmost in service.

UNION MADE Lee

The World's Largest Manufacturers
on-Made Work Clothing

THE H. D. L

B.F.Go TIRES·B

Lee UNION MADE WORK CLOTHES

accumulated over the past half century or so, it wouldn't pay to flood the market.

Even as these modern-day treasure hunters scavenged the back roads of America for more, Tokyo had become the planetary Mecca for vintage denim buyers and sellers. An estimated 2,000 tons of vintage and contemporary denim were finding their way to Japan every year, and it was not enough. As long as the yen stayed strong, masses of Japanese youths flocked to stores stocked to the ceiling with rare and vintage American denim. Most of the customers were and are well informed about vintage. They had better be. Some of the most rare vintage Levi's 501s were selling for thousands of dollars (not yen), with older jackets commanding even higher prices. There were subtle distinctions in these old jeans, but those subtleties meant a big difference in value and price, and, of course, they meant a big difference in status. Beyond a fad, that was what the denim phenomenon was about. Status.

To most Americans, jeans are jeans. Levi 501s are Levi's 501s. A Lee Storm Rider jacket is a Lee Storm Rider jacket. As long as they are not too worn out, Americans don't care if they were made in 1940 or 1990. They were, on the surface at least, the same jeans Americans grew up in and the same jeans their fathers wore. Otherwise, not many distinct differences exist.

However, this is not true of collectors, aficionados, and buyers and sellers of vintage denim. It is the subtle differences and the rarity of these old garments that makes one pair an old Buick and another a Deusenberg. It is the same with most collectible objects. There are always different levels of collectors with varying levels of interest, passion for collecting, and knowledge about collecting, buying, and selling.

From the increasing amount of press that this vintage denim phenomenon has

received, many people know that old jeans are worth something. And many know what "Big E" Levi jeans are. For those who don't, the Big E refers to the little red cloth tab Levi Strauss and Company added to their 501 jeans and most other Levi's pants beginning in 1936. The little red tab sewn into the side seam of the right-hand back pocket simply reads "LEVI'S." It read this way until 1971

Ron and Cindy Wright of Denver, Colorado, in front of their vintage store Boss Unlimited.

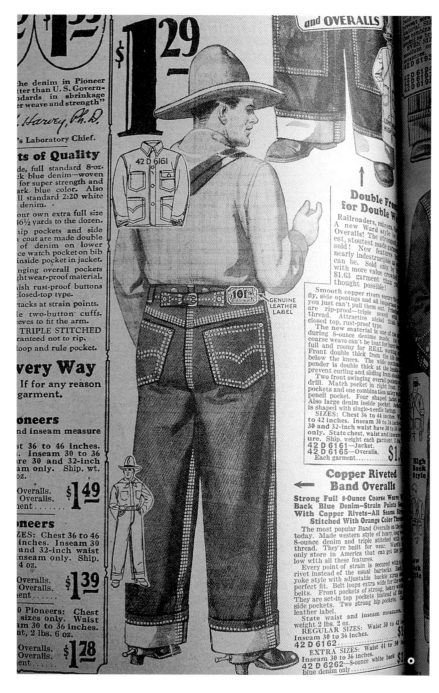

serious business with serious dollars involved.

Like any antique, collectible, or most businesses for that matter, it is difficult to get the sellers involved to talk about money and value of vintage denim. Until recently, there hasn't even been a printed price guide available. There was a sort of unwritten price guide that most dealers in vintage denim adhered to, at least within some reasonable proximity to each other. Successful buying and selling of vintage denim meant it couldn't be too overpriced or underpriced. As with most commodities, supply and demand would establish value and rarity, and condition would help to determine price. It is safe to say there are certain Japanese and some, though fewer, Americans who have made considerable sums of money in buying and selling used denim. Some have even become millionaires. But that is not the norm. The cream on top of the milk bottle is very thin, and in the complex equation of trading in this strange commodity, there isn't room for everyone to become rich. However, Levi Strauss and Company estimates two-and-a-half-billion pairs of denim pants have been made since Levi Strauss made his first pair back in 1853. So, it would seem logical that there ought to be lots of old pants out there that will be worth some money.

Early catalogs such as this vintage Cheyenne Outfitters catalog are a good resource to help identify vintage denim garments.

when that little red tab was altered to read "LeVI'S." The distinctions are subtle in the vintage denim world. All that changed was the lowering of the letter "E" in the tab from being a Big E to a little, or lower-case, "e." What the subtle distinction means is that two almost identical garments, one with a Big E tag and one without, will vary in price so that the Big E is likely going to be worth at least twice and maybe ten times as much (or more) than the garment with the lower-case "e." It could mean the difference between having a real Rolex watch or buying a cheap knockoff. To many buyers/collectors, it's

Vintage 501s from the thirties. The red tab on the pocket of Levi's jeans and jackets can be one of the most obvious clues to vintage denim hunters. The Big E, or capital E, on vintage-denim garments was changed to a lower-case letter "e" in the early 1970s.

JUST WHERE IS THAT DUSTY DENIM?
THE TREASURE HUNT
PICKERS AND SCOUTS

When word got out that a single Levi denim jacket from the early 1940s sold recently for $5,000 or that a similar but earlier Lee jacket changed hands for $40,000, or that a pair of early buckle-back 501s might sell for more than $30,000, people noticed. No one knows for sure how many people are in this weird business full-time, or how many people do it as a sideline, or how many buyers those people have out there looking for them. These buyers, called "pickers" in the trade, are the true hunters. For many, it is an everyday treasure hunt that leads them through the dusty garages, basements, and attics of people having garage or yard sales. "Tag sales," as they are called in some parts of the country, are probably the best chance a beginner might have to luck onto a true piece of vintage American denim. As far as other possibilities—thrift stores, charity stores, second-hand and antique stores—there is too much awareness about the value in old denim for most people in those businesses not to know about the worth of old jeans, jackets, and shirts. They may not know the subtleties, but they won't put them out on the rack for a few dollars like they did ten years ago. And most of those shops have regulars for whom they set aside old denim, or who will come look at the store's new vintage merchandise on a daily basis.

If just a single pair of older Big E jeans could bring a picker hundreds or thousands of dollars, it sometimes becomes lucrative to stake out the local Salvation Army or Goodwill store and be right there when last night's donations are wheeled out onto the sales floor. It happens in more than a dozen thrift stores in Denver alone. This waiting, like buzzards circling for dead denim, is a full-time job for many of these people. It may seem strange, but

A modern-day prospector mines for blue gold while looking through piles of vintage denim at the Rose Bowl flea market in Pasadena, California.

some of them are getting lucky, and some are making a very good living. Still, pickers, scouts, and buyers can't be everywhere all the time. Maybe they don't know about a church sale or about the neighbor's yard sale.

Newspapers now carry dozens of advertisements from those eager to buy denim. Most of these people are denim wholesalers who buy jeans and other collectible denim over the counter and either hold that merchandise until their buyer comes or pack it up and send it to their overseas buyers. The demand is still primarily in Japan, but there has always been a strong market for American denim in England, France, Germany, and other European countries. Lately, other Asian countries have begun to import denim, especially Thailand. In Denver alone, there are probably a hundred small storefronts, which have sprung up like corner grocery stores, that offer to buy used jeans, primarily Levi's 501s. These are the "gold standard" in the secondhand jeans

business, but other brands are collectible and valuable, too. Wrangler, Lee, and some of the smaller but now defunct brands of denim clothing are also in demand. The demand often changes according to supply, what is popular at the moment in Japan, or the value of the yen. The recent economic troubles in Japan have somewhat slowed down the vintage trade despite its trendiness; American jeans are still considered a luxury, not a necessity. But trading continues, and no one seems to know when it will end. If it were a fad, it should have ended ten years ago. Some Japanese have been importing American blue jeans for almost two decades now, and rumors say some Japanese shop owners have warehouses with enough vintage denim to keep the market going for another decade. One thing probably is true: chances are good there is more vintage American denim in Japan than there is in America.

In many small towns, especially in the

West and Midwest, traveling buyers will set up shop for a few days and advertise locally to buy used denim. These jeans gypsies often do quite well because they are in markets where there might not be any awareness of the value of older denim, and they are in a location where much of the denim has been worn for many years. Also, farm and ranch people generally don't throw much away. There is still a depression mentality in many of these small rural towns, because for many people there, the Great Depression was a time that really tested them, their parents, or grandparents. Because most of them still make their living from the land, the threat of another depression is not nearly as remote a possibility as it is for other Americans. Consequently, things out on the ranch or farm have value even if they aren't needed today. "Someday" they might need that item, so they'd better keep it. Most farms and ranches are home to dozens of old cars, tractors, plows, wagons—heaps of junk that look totally worthless. Car collectors have known this for years, and some travel the country with flatbed trucks, buying up classic, restorable automobiles from these folks' junk piles.

It is many a junk dealer's dream to get into the barns, sheds, and attics of these old farms and ranch houses. Somewhere out there is another Lee jacket with donut "Cowboy" buttons that didn't quite fit Grandpa and was put away in new condition fifty years ago. They are out there. Even the most diligent Japanese denim divers can't look in every old trunk, and for many nationals, their foreignness keeps them from getting to those treasures locked away in the attics and cellars of rural America.

As for finding the real mother lode of denim-blue gold—the basement of an old store that went out of business during the depression and has never re-opened or the warehouse full of fifties jeans jackets that just

didn't sell—that is about as difficult and rare as digging out a large gold nugget from an abandoned gold mine. For the most part, unfortunately, someone's already been there. As the value of just about anything old or antique has climbed steadily in the past few years, those basements and boarded-up stores were opened up to collectors and pickers who, if they had any sense, probably bought up everything in sight, including the old store advertising. Be it wooden, glass, electric, neon, or cardboard—any sign or any advertising that advertised Lee, Levi, Wrangler, or other denim brands is practically worth its weight in gold. The writer of a 1994 *Esquire* magazine article on denim said that

The merchandising of used denim has spawned storefronts such as this one in hundreds of American towns and cities.

at a Paris auction in 1992, a Levi's promotional item from the 1940s—a pair of 501s on a cardboard cowboy—sold for about $75,000. Almost any antique advertising material is collectible in this country, but denim advertising sets the pace as far as value is concerned, partly because not a lot of it was produced in the early days.

A promotional item that was fairly common was novelty garments, mostly jeans, that were made either in giant or miniature sizes. Accurate and authentic in almost every detail as their regular garments, jeans manufacturers made these enormous pants to hang on store walls or to hang outside a storefront. Also, they made Lilliputian-sized pants as store giveaways to promote their particular brand of pants to customers. While still valuable, these more mass-produced items aren't as valuable as promotional items designed for in-store use. Unless a seller knows some giants or six-inch-tall buyers, these garments aren't worth as much as their counterparts that were made at the same time in a wearable size.

Size is just one of the many considerations when determining the value of a vintage denim garment. For the most part, buyers of vintage denim want to buy merchandise that can be worn. Some items may be too rare and valuable to be worn, or their condition might be too fragile to withstand wearing, but even very old denim will be worn if it is wearable. So, buyers will look for the following criteria in selecting denim to buy:

AGE OF THE GARMENT

As with any collectible, this is one of the primary criteria to determine value. And, as with most collectibles, the older the better and more valuable. Age can be determined by several style clues in most garments. In earlier denim garments, the way the denim was loomed differs from much of today's denim. Further clues such as red lines, buckle backs, Big E tags, and others help to determine the article's age and worth.

Turn up the cuff on a pair of Levi's jeans. If there is a visible red line along the seam, you have a pair of vintage pre-1985 Levi's.

RED LINES

Do the jeans have a white strip, about a half inch wide, visible on the inside of the leg seams? This is selvage, the edge of a woven fabric designed to keep it from unraveling. The white selvage is a giveaway to a pair of pants that most likely was loomed prior to the 1980s. Does it have a red thread on the inside of the leg seams? That red stripe disappeared on 501s in 1986. These pre-1990s Levi's have become the hot item as the really rare, older vintage denim has disappeared into collectors' closets around the world. Known as "Red Lines" or *Akamimi,* meaning "red ear" in Japanese, these pants can be readily identified from the outside by the black stitching at the top corners of the back pockets. Known to collectors and vintage hunters as "Black Flag," this stitching further identifies red lines that are worth almost twice as much on the market as are regular contemporary 501s. This particular kind of selvage also creates a slightly raised section of material along the outside seam.

Wearable sizes of vintage-denim clothing generally makes them more valuable, but if original tags are still intact and the garment was never worn, size is not as important because the garment probably won't be worn but kept in original condition.

After several washings, this raised section, called "tracks," because it resembles railroad tracks, becomes obvious when it fades more quickly than the rest of the garment. For whatever reasons, used Levis with tracking are in high demand, especially in Thailand. In 1995, red lines were the jeans of choice for most buyers. They are vintage but not so old that they can't be found in large quantities. Even though only less than ten years old, red lines command as much as $200 a pair in most foreign markets.

BIG Es

Another way to determine the age of a pair of Levi's, the Big E or Capital E is a clue to age. The Big E red tab is located on the side of the right back pocket of Levi's jeans and on the side of the left breast pocket on most Levi jackets. If the little red tab reads LeVI'S, it was most likely made after 1971. If the red tab bears a Big E in its LEVI'S logo, you are holding some real vintage denim manufactured somewhere between 1936 and 1971. Prices for these Capital E Levi products vary greatly depending on other factors such as age, condition, rarity, color, size, and demand. Vintage denim should be shopped around to different potential buyers for the best price. As a ballpark guide, most Big E's in good condition that are sold in Japan will bring a minimum of $400. Sellers to American buyers should expect to receive one-fourth to one-half of its final selling value in Japan.

These first subtle clues helped determine age for Levi's-brand vintage denim. The following clues apply to other brand names of collectible and vintage denim:

RIVETS

Rivets, their location, and how they're stamped also are clues to vintage denim value. Experienced Levi's buyers can date some garments simply from what letter or numeral is stamped on the back of a rivet. Early Levi's had rivets on the back pockets. These disappeared in 1936, supposedly in response to school boards complaining to Levi Strauss that the copper rivets on the backs of jeans were tearing up chairs on school desks. Rivets on the back pockets of most denim jeans likely indicate that they predate 1937. Levi's jeans that came out after 1937 had hidden rivets. These "concealed rivets," as the company called them, were hidden on the inside of the pocket until double stitching replaced them in the early sixties. A good-condition pair of "concealed copper rivet" Levi's may be worth several thousand dollars in overseas markets.

The copper crotch rivet that used to be on Levi's 501s, Lee jeans, and other denim pants, disappeared around World War II after many complaints and, as mentioned previously, the crotch branding of Walter Haas Sr., then-president of Levi Strauss and Company.

RARITY

How rare is this garment? Were many made? Did many survive? This is tough information to come by, and it's not getting easier. Major manufacturers of denim, especially Levi Strauss and Company, have been deluged with calls and letters from denim collectors seeking information. Because of the counterfeiting of many of their vintage garments and advertising, Levi Strauss and Company is beginning to be very cautious with vintage denim sellers and collectors. Partly due to this overwhelming interest and partly due to a lack of information, it is difficult to determine just how rare a vintage denim garment might be. The marketplace

will inevitably decide. What might be in demand now and worth hundreds may be worthless tomorrow. Hoarding vintage denim, then, may be a mistake.

CONDITION

What is the overall condition of the garment? Was it ever worn? Is it dead stock with the original labels or packaging intact? How worn is it? If it has been washed and faded, how even is the fading? How dark is the color? In today's markets, color or degree of fading has a lot to do with pricing and also with where the vintage denim is ultimately marketed. Japanese buyers seem to prefer a deeper blue color with less fade. Europeans, Greeks, Italians, and others prefer a very faded, overall, light-blue look. Was it dyed with real indigo dye? Older fabrics, especially those used in 501 Big E jeans, keep a darker,

Savvy collectors will take it upon themselves to learn everything they can about identifying vintage garments, including the smallest of details such as the stamping on rivets or the location of rivets on the garment.

Color and degree of fade also affect the value and market for used and vintage denim. Some dealers and buyers, as well as customers, prefer a certain degree of fade in the vintage they buy.

Right: An early Lee Riders advertising piece that was given away to customers. The bowleggedness of the garment depicted is perhaps an allusion to the cowboy-pant origins of Lee jeans.

more grainy blue color than contemporary jeans. The differences are most obvious if the two garments are side by side. For a seasoned buyer or picker, the older, darker indigo fabric will stand out on a rack of a hundred jeans. It's all a matter of education.

Does it have many holes? How big are the holes? Does it have any rips, tears, or open seams? Can it be sewn back together? Is there enough usable materials on the garment that it can be used for parts? (Yes, jeans sellers do "part out" some vintage denim jackets to make another piece whole again). Are all of the buttons there? Is the original label still intact and legible? Has the garment been written on, or painted on, or had patches sewn on it? Is it repairable? These are all good questions to ask when hunting for vintage denim.

SIZE

Is it a good size? What is a "good size," anyway? Average size is generally important when looking at vintage denim that will be sold to be worn. Denim buyers will generally only buy pants that meet certain waist and length (inseam) sizes. But that could change almost weekly. In years past, most buyers for the Japanese market wouldn't purchase a waist size larger than thirty-eight or thirty-six. But as those "desirable waist sizes" disappeared, the "baggy pants" and "hip-hop" look of very large pants became popular in Japan. Nowadays, large waist sizes command more than their smaller-waisted brothers and sisters. Different sizes also are shipped to different markets.

Very long or very short inseams are usually not as desirable. A lot of vintage denim that has survived in good condition did so because it was an unusual size—either very large or very small—and probably didn't sell well in those sizes. Some of these very large or very small garments may still be worth a

great deal because of their good condition and their rarity; but generally, the medium-sized garments will have the most value to a buyer. The larger-sized pants usually will be going to markets in Europe or England.

BRAND

As previously stated, Levi's 501s are the gold standard for denim buyers. It is the most sought after and the most widely purchased garment at both wholesale and retail levels. The same can be said for Levi's denim jackets; they are the ones most consistently in demand in overseas markets even though Lee jackets are more valuable, with Wrangler brand next and other brands coming in behind that.

As in the requirements for pants, many of the same criteria apply for judging the value of a jacket and its desirability. Other things to look for in jackets are whether they are lined or unlined and the condition of the

lining. Newer vintage jackets have a different type of blanket lining than older jackets. Also, most new jackets have side pockets that are not as desirable, marking the jacket as a contemporary garment. Check the labels carefully. Look for that Big E tab to help date a jacket. Generally, denim jackets with a

Levi's have become bigger than life in this art piece painted on the floor of the Worn Out West vintage store in Hollywood.

Below left: An early Wrangler rear-pocket label showing the Blue Bell logo above, an obvious clue to a valuable pair of vintage Wrangler jeans.

A buckle on the back of a pair of vintage jeans or vintage-jeans jacket usually means the garment will bring a lot of money to a fortunate vintage scout. It generally is a dead giveaway that a denim garment is vintage.

single breast pocket and a buckle cinch in back are the earlier jackets and are worth more. Some of these early jackets are hanging on hangers in vintage shops, sporting four- and five-digit price tags.

Early Levi's jackets date back to the 1920s. Labels might be marked with a style number ranging from 213 for some of the first jackets to 506XX for the 1938 model. These jackets often had "donut-hole" buttons, as opposed to the solid buttons of newer jackets. They generally had only four buttons on the front and a single, flapless pocket. Buttons that were embossed with a leaf wreath around the button or donut-hole buttons that had Levi Strauss and Company and a small star embossed on the button were the earliest.

Another identifying mark on vintage jackets can be found on the label, also known as the neck tag, sewn inside the back of the jacket and centered below the collar. Early

jackets might be marked with a 213 or a 506XX for the 1938 model. This model can be distinguished by a silver buckle on the cinch in the back, too. A silver buckle is older and more valuable than a bronze-colored buckle. The 506XX is often referred to as a "first" jacket by dealers and collectors. It will sport rivets on the front pocket and a rivet about six inches above the cuff. In addition, early jackets were cut square in the back with no tapering seams as seen in more modern jackets.

The 507XX Levi's jacket has silver buttons and a pleated placket on both sides of the buttons. These jackets are referred to as "seconds." A lot number 517 denotes a lined jacket. Occasionally, a 507BXX label will be found. This simply indicates the jacket is a boy's size. Generally, youth sizes in pants and jackets are not as valuable.

Following a second jacket in age and value is an indigo-dyed, two-pocket jacket

Although it is a rarity,
there are still many
denim garments out
there that can be worth
thousands of dollars in
the vintage market.

that will have a tapered back and front and a little "e" red tab on the left chest pocket. The color and the weave of this jacket from the late sixties and early seventies is different than contemporary jackets.

Lee denim jackets are fairly easy to date since they have three styles of pocket tags, and two of these tags are considered vintage. The oldest tag on jackets made until the 1960s, located on the left chest pocket on the label in back, will simply read "Lee." After the 1960s, the tag changed to read "Lee" with a small circled "R" to the bottom right of the last "e" in Lee. In the 1970s, the tag was changed again with the letters "M.R." appearing above a circled letter "R."

Lee's buckle-back cowboy jacket was made from the 1930s until World War II. It has one pocket, and the words "Union Made" are embossed on the buttons. Lee jackets are often the exception to the Levi's-beats-Lee rule of pricing. Early Lee jackets are usually worth more because Lee produced fewer of them than Levi Strauss and Company produced.

Lee cowboy jackets, style number 101J, from 1945 to the early fifties, are also a good vintage find. These jackets have two pockets, and the buckle back has disappeared. The label in the back is black with a yellow "Lee." Red stitching on this label reads "Union Made Sanforized."

From the mid-fifties to the early sixties, Lee's jacket tag read "Union Made Lee Sanforized—Lot 101J" and included the size and words "Design Patented" with a patent number. The buttons were embossed with "Lee Rider." Another rarer tag from this time period is triangular and increases the value of the jacket. A lined jacket from this time period carried the style number 101LJ and was called "Storm Rider" because the label depicted a cowboy on horseback in a snowstorm.

Between 1962 and 1970, a white tag with gold embroidery thread on a black label displayed the circled "R" registered trademark for the first time. This jacket is similar in age and value to a Levi Big E jacket. Jackets from the early seventies returned to a simple neck tag that read "Lee" with the circled "R" and the letters "M.R." Underneath that is the word "Sanforized," a patent number, and the words "Union Made in the U.S.A."

Like the Lee and Levi's jackets, early model Wrangler jackets were buckle backs, with two buckles in the back and two pleats down the front held together by yellow- or gold-colored embroidered dots. Early jackets also had elastic straps inside the jacket to allow for a better, more adaptive fit. These jackets feature two hand pockets on the front and one pocket on the left chest that has a flap. Usually this jacket has a zipper instead of buttons, and the neck tag reads "WRANGLER" with a Blue Bell logo directly above. In fact, the Blue Bell logo appears on all vintage Wrangler clothing.

Wrangler made denim in other colors as well, including white, brown, and different shades of blue. Colored and white denim are in demand but not as valuable as the standard blue denim. Other colored jackets have not yet found any popularity with most collectors. Acid-washed, stonewashed, or bleached jackets, like the pants, are generally not collectible.

The one detail that applies to all denim jackets is that unlined jackets are worth more than lined jackets. Blanket-lined jackets are worth more than fleece-lined jackets, which some dealers won't buy at all. Also, many newer jackets have side pockets that are not as desirable and generally mark the jacket as a contemporary garment.

Beyond its standard jackets and pants, Levi Strauss and Company has entered the marketplace with a wide variety of clothing styles and fabrics, as well as a myriad of other products labeled "Levi's" in its more than a hundred

years of manufacturing. These have included laundry bags, place mats, notebooks, binders, shoes, hats; they even had their name on a car. American Motors introduced one of its vehicles outfitted with Levi's denim upholstery. Other denim manufacturers as well have made many different garments and products throughout their histories, and most of those might be collectible now.

Not many rules and guidelines apply to hunting vintage denim. It is where buyers find it—if they are lucky enough to be there first. As is true in almost any field of collecting, knowledge is the best asset. The one who knows the most about vintage denim will most likely be the one who finds the most of it. Vintage denim, perhaps worth thousands of dollars, may sit, totally ignored at a garage sale while eager antique hunters fight over a two-dollar sugar bowl or a broken doll. Knowing even a little bit about vintage denim clothing gives a person an advantage over most other treasure hunters. Vintage denim is still a very new phenomenon, at least in this country, and most ordinary folk are incredulous when told some of the amounts of money old jeans have brought to the lucky finders. As a collectible, vintage denim is still a sleeper in this country. But this is changing rapidly with the appearance of books on vintage clothing and denim, magazine articles on the value of vintage denim, and news-feature stories on the phenomenon of collectible blue jeans and jackets. It appears denim is hotter than ever.

Once-common denim clothing is now displayed like high fashion or fine art in a gallery in many vintage shops across the country.

THE FUTURE OF DENIM
NEW BLUES

Denim is everywhere. If it weren't for denim, a good portion of the world's population might be running around naked . . . or worse, they might still be wearing polyester or some other synthetic fabric. As we approach the dawn of the twenty-first century, denim, an ages-old cotton cloth, is still the fabric of choice for millions, and it shows no sign of diminishing in popularity. In fact, quite the contrary. What once was the symbol of rebellion and recklessness has now become mainstream and more common than Coca-Cola. What once thumbed its nose at fashion, now is a fashion staple. Look through any American or European fashion magazine. What do you see? Denim. The classic blue-jeans look is re-invented every fashion season, taking on new life in garments never dreamed of by the early makers of denim work clothes.

It's difficult to improve upon something that has worked so well for more than a hundred years, but manufacturers are trying to apply the high-tech future to denim. Levi Strauss and Company has introduced computer technology to its jeans buyers. In selected parts of the country, sales clerks at an Original Levi's Store use a computer and a customer's vital statistics to create "perfect-fitting blue jeans"—in essence, a digital blue-jeans blueprint. Levi's "Personal Pair" program has expanded its jeans options for women from 170 combinations of sizes and shapes to 4,224. No more digging through racks, carrying armloads of jeans, and making dozens of trips to the dressing room. After about ten minutes and a few measurements, size information is transmitted electronically to a Levi's factory in Tennessee where a computer directs a

Mirrored in the chrome of a vintage Harley-Davidson, a pair of denim pants could bring a lucky finder enough money to buy his own antique motorcycle. Like many other collectibles, vintage denim is increasing in value because it is increasing in popularity and rarity.

Harley-Davidson has joined the ranks of hundreds of other denim manufacturers with its own brand of denim clothing, called "Biker Blues," aimed at the growing biker market.

robotics tailor to cut a pair of jeans precisely to match the woman's measurements. The finished product reportedly sells for only about $10 more than a pair of Levi's off the shelf and can be in the customer's hands in a matter of weeks. For an extra five bucks, Levi Strauss and Company will ship directly to the customer. And once measured, the customer is given an identification number to order additional pairs with a simple phone call. So far, the made-to-order Levi's are for women only and are being offered in only a few major, mostly eastern, cities. The company reports its plans to offer the service at more than thirty Original Levi's Stores throughout the country by the end of 1995. This could be the start of a trend that the clothing industry calls "mass customization," where customers can get a mass-marketed article of clothing that will be computer fit exactly for them.

A recent Lands' End clothing company catalog was titled *The Denim Yarns*, and the whole catalog concept paid homage to the role of denim as a "true blue friend." Numerous designers have come out with complete collections based on denim, from clothing to bed sheets to curtains. Stores exclusively devoted to denim have sprung up around the country. One such company, The Denim Works, has opened three retail stores in Denver in the past year. Harley-Davidson has celebrated the affinity bikers have always had for blue jeans and denim with its own line of denim clothing, "Biker Blues," and by creating a denim motorcycle to promote its line of denim. As America has loosened its corporate neckties and dress codes, denim and jeans are again work clothes, but they are going to work in offices instead of on the streets and railroads. Levi Strauss and Company publishes a newsletter, "Casual Clothing in the Workplace," in response to more than 8,000 United States corporations,

including eighty-one of the top Fortune 500 that have contacted Levi Strauss for "information and guidance on how to introduce casual business wear to the workplace." Yes, corporate America has to learn from another corporation how to dress down. Thousands of American businesses, even including the CIA, have loosened up—at least on Fridays—when many businesses have opted to dispense with dark suits and ties or a dress

Denim jeans stand alone as a sexy fashion item that has stayed in fashion for decades.

code that required at least a semiformal appearance. Employees across the country are being encouraged to dress casually in the workplace, with many companies easing into the trend by allowing casual dress one day a week. Rick Bragg of the *New York Times* said, "Marketing experts call it a megatrend in corporate dressing." In that same *New York Times* story on casual dress in the workplace, A. Wright Elliot of the Chase Manhattan Bank said, "The outside world prefers to deal with relaxed, genuinely cheerful workers, and that's good for business." American big business is finding out what most of us have known all along: when we are comfortable, we are happier. When we are wearing our jeans, we are comfortable. Inspiration usually comes from a relaxed state of mind, and jeans are what we relax in. America could be on to a whole new surge of business productivity and creativity as we

Another generation grows up in jeans, ensuring the continued popularity of denim clothing.

Vintage advertising such as this Lee metal sign will continue to climb in value and serve as a landmark to the history of denim.

UNION MADE GUARANTEED
Lee
OVERALLS

now button up our jeans to go to work.

Perhaps this trend toward more relaxed clothing and the incredible growth of denim clothing has something to do with the growing interest in vintage denim. Maybe America is gaining some reverence for jeans and jackets that lived through times past. Maybe we are thinking we must be missing something when the Palais Galliera in Paris hosts the world's first exhibition devoted to the history of jeans.

Vintage denim won't be a new concept in America much longer. In July of 1994, *Esquire* magazine ran a ten-page fashion section in tribute to denim, "its history, its lore, its technology, and its place in the culture." It also earned the ire of many denim hunters and wholesalers by printing, for the first time in a major national magazine, information on the value of vintage and collectible denim and how to go about identifying and finding it.

Many dealers want to keep this information secret. And why not? If someone sees their sign to BUY LEVIS and brings in a pair of buckle-backed Levis from the 1930s, chances are good the seller doesn't know

what he has or what it could be worth. He leaves with the ten or twenty dollars the wholesaler pays and is happy. The wholesaler now has a pair of vintage jeans worth maybe three thousand dollars. He is very happy. Knowledge is power, and in this case, knowledge is money, so many dealers don't want the public knowing about vintage denim. The other concern is that once it is widely known, the market will be flooded with vintage denim garments, and prices will plummet. Nevertheless, dealers can't keep this information to themselves forever. Fashion giant *Vogue* magazine came out with an article on vintage denim ("Rags to Riches: Are Your Jeans Worth $10,000?") in its April 1995 issue. In its article "The Denim Standard," *Vogue's* writer traveled the vintage denim trail from Missoula, Montana, to the Rose Bowl in Pasadena, California, to downtown Bangkok in Thailand. It's almost like reading about an illicit international drug deal, this strange dealing in old blue denim.

But some dealers in denim welcome the spread of information and the unveiling of the "secrets" of the denim trade. Some such

As comfortable as an old pair of boots, vintage-denim clothing has spawned an interest in other vintage clothing and collectibles such as these motorcycle and cowboy boots.

as John Farley of Orem, Utah, even openly share their secrets in hopes of becoming a major dealer to those with whom he shares his information on denim and other vintage collectibles. Farley has even produced a slick sixty-page color magazine that tells vintage hunters in great detail what to look for and

how to find vintage denim. The magazine is bilingual—half of it is printed in English, half in Japanese. The Japanese section explains to its readers how to come to America to find their own vintage clothing. He highlights one city per issue with maps and guides to all the popular American thrift stores such as the

Goodwill, Salvation Army, Disabled American Veterans, Savers, and others. Farley said he isn't very popular with other vintage denim wholesalers and harbors some concern that others might do anything to stop him. It's a big business with lots of money involved when simple competition for old pants

mushrooms into a fear that competitors might want to kill you. Over a pair of pants? No, not exactly, though people in this country have been killed for their athletic shoes and jackets. It's not over a single pair of pants but over an underground business that mostly deals in cash and lots of it. Even a small portion of the overseas vintage denim business has brought many young dealers incredible wealth, and they are anxious to protect their golden goose.

The golden goose of vintage denim is getting to be a very busy bird. Though not exactly vintage, used Levi's 501s have been showing up for sale in the oddest places— Bloomingdales in Chicago, for instance, where a saleswoman said they "just can't keep them in." Down the street from Bloomingdales, the same used, faded blue Levi's 501s are for sale to a younger, hipper crowd than Bloomingdale's usually attracts. Urban Outfitters is a chain of very with-it clothing stores geared toward what some call Generation Xers. But it's no small business. Urban Outfitters has about twenty stores across America and does a booming business in used Levi's.

Across the street from Chicago's Urban Outfitters, another chic, youth-oriented store also has used Levi's stacked up for sale. Boogie's Diner, whose original store was in trendy, expensive Aspen, Colorado, has piles

of faded, worn and torn, used Levi's for sale underneath a vintage Harley-Davidson motorcycle, neon signs, and expensive leather biker jackets. What's strange is, it no longer looks unusual to see stacks of used pants for sale in an upscale clothing store. There are dozens of shops along cool Melrose Avenue in Hollywood that specialize in selling used denim—mostly worn, modern, Levi's 501s. But here, perhaps more than anywhere in the United States, can be found a wide assortment of expensive vintage denim clothing. Denim, leather, and spandex are the Melrose uniforms. Summer comes and jeans cutoffs get shorter every year. Every August in Sturgis, South Dakota, close to a half-million bikers come to town in an annual pilgrimage and tribute to the biker lifestyle. Denim and black leather meet chrome and steel and meld together in the classic biker look. Hot August days here mean jeans cut-offs for many bikers' "old ladies," and they often show more skin than denim as cutoffs get cut so short that they sometimes become G-strings with pockets.

Other denim-related items such as this vintage Levi Strauss belt buckle are also collectible and becoming quite valuable.

IDENTIFYING VINTAGE DENIM

VINTAGE 501 LEVI'S

1 RED LINES:

Known to the Japanese as *akamimi's,* red lines are the newest vintage Levi's. Red lines get their name from the two red lines that run on the inside of the outside seam. As the Levi's are washed, these lines turn pink; however, they still are considered red lines. Two categories of red lines exist—single stitch and double stitch. Single-stitch red lines are older than double stitch and have a greater value.

STITCHING:
Double stitch are the most common red lines. They get their name from the double stitching along the inside

Double stitch

Single stitch

top of the back pockets. Be sure to check the inside of the back pocket; from the outside, single-stitch and double-stitch red lines look identical.

SEAM:
Tracks run down both sides of the outer seam and consist of a slightly raised section of material that measures approxi-

mately three-quarters of an inch wide. Raising is caused by overlapping material on the inside of the seam called the selvage. Since this part of the garment is raised, the faded tracks are easy to spot.

BUTTON:
You can differentiate single-stitch from double-stitch red lines by the top fly button. If three numbers are stamped on the back of the button, the Levi's are double stitch. Single-stitch Levi's have a single-digit number stamped on the back of the button.

POCKETS:
Most red lines are identified by the black stitching

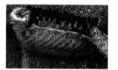

located at the top corners of the back pockets.

LITTLE e TAG
Red lines are the only vintage jeans with a little "e" tag.

CUFF:
An older pair of single-stitch Levi's has yellow stitching around the cuff instead of the traditional copper-color stitch. If you find these variations in a pair of Levi's, you have found yourself a pair of vintage red lines.

Red-line seam

2 BIG E:

The next stage in vintage Levi's is big E, named for the capital E on the red pocket tag. Similar to red lines, big E Levi's are divided into two categories. The first is the 501 big E. This is the same as the single-stitch red line, except for the capital E. The next category is 501A, 501F (failure) or 501S big E with two-tone stitching. The major variation in this category is the stitched V that appears near the back of the top fly button.

STITCHED V:

Next to the top fly button, check for v-shaped stitching. Big E Levi's were stitched this way until 1968.

TWO-TONE STITCHING:

On the back pockets and cuffs, check for yellow and copper-colored stitching. Two-tone stitching ended in 1967.

501A:
Grade A material. 1966–68.

501S:
Satisfactory material. 1966–68.

BIG E TAG
Notice the capital letters. Levi stopped making big "Es" in 1971.

Vintage Levi's follow a similar grading system to used 501s; however, size is critical to vintage items. Waist size and inseam must range thirty-two inches or larger. The denim must be dark—minimal fading. Although any vintage item is worth a great deal, vintage in top condition is best.

3   501XX:

The 501XX stage of vintage Levi's has the greatest number of variations. Only the slightest distinctions separate each category.

Lot 501XX:

The difference between the first 501XXs and big E Levi's is the tag between the back belt loops. While big E's have "501," the 501XX has the word "Lot" before the number and "XX" after the number. Used 501s of today also have "XX" on the tag. Check for red lines; all vintage Levi's have red lines.

Hidden Rivets:

The next 501XX has hidden rivets that fasten the back pockets to the jeans. Later, Levi pockets were stitched together. The rivets are visible from the inside, not the outside.

Paper Tag:

This tag is found on vintage and non-vintage 501XXs. Identify paper-tag vintage by red lines or hidden rivets. 1960–65.

Paper Tag with Guarantee:

This is the last paper tag. On the tag is written: "Every Garment Guaranteed." This category also has hidden rivets. 1954–60.

Leather Tag:

The tag on this category of Levi's is leather; it's the only difference between the previous category. 1943–55

4 WORLD WAR II XX:

In World War II, Levi Strauss didn't use his traditional pocket stitching logo on his jeans. Instead, the insignia was painted on. This difference creates a stage all its own.

5 DONUT HOLE:

About the same time World War II XXs were produced, donut-hole buttons were used (notice the hollow center). Another Levi stage was born.

EARLY LOGO:
Levi Strauss & Company stamped its name on buttons from 1922 to 1936. During World War II, the company went to a cheaper leaf logo.

LEAF LOGO:
Generic buttons are cheaper than custom-designed buttons. Donut-hole buttons ended in 1947.

ONE-SIDED STITCHING:
World War II pocket tabs had white stitching on one side. This was changed in 1950.

PAINTED STICHING:
To save thread during World War II, back-pocket stitching was painted on.

6 BUCKLE BACKS:

The last vintage stage is buckle backs. Similar characteristics exist in this stage's two categories. Buckle backs get their name from the pant's silver buckle and denim belt, which is secured by copper rivets.

A copper-crotch rivet always accompanies buckle backs. If you see a crotch rivet, you've found something valuable. Exposed copper rivets attach the back pockets. The rivets were concealed eventually by a layer of fabric, and today the pockets are secured with stitching.

Back-pocket Levi's insignias were sewn by hand. This is easily seen because the lines are not parallel or symmetrical. The absence or presence of belt loops differentiates buckle-back categories.

BELT LOOPS:
Belt loops were included with buckle backs and replaced the suspender buttons. The buckle back impedes the use of a belt.

CROTCH RIVET:
Buckle backs included a crotch rivet.

NO BELT LOOPS:
The first buckle backs had no belt loops. Instead, buttons were provided to attach suspenders.

EXPOSED RIVETS:
This rare pocket features exposed rivets.

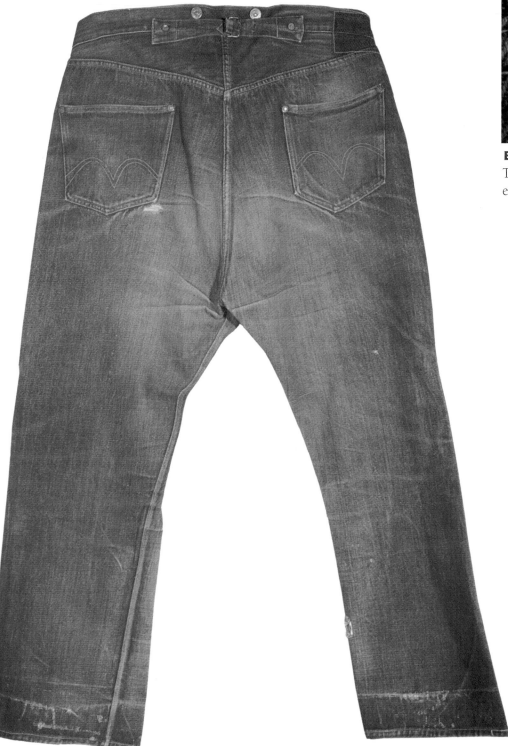

HOW TO IDENTIFY VINTAGE LEE JEANS:

Many people overlook vintage Lee and Wrangler jeans because there isn't a market for their nonvintage varieties. Lee and Wrangler vintage items have value and sell well in Japan. Don't neglect them in your search.

1 AROUND 1889

H. D. Lee General Trading Company was established in Kansas City. About 1912, Lee started manufacturing Lee bib overalls and work jackets. The trademark was "Union All." The Lee Company made trademark brand names, including "Logan Jeans."

Around 1924, cowboy jeans—cowboy pants in those days—were similar to the original style of modern Lee Riders, but they were more like work pants than jeans.

2 AROUND 1936

Lee jeans started to develop into the modern jeans of today. Lee buckle backs, more commonly known as Lee Cowboy jeans with a buckle in the back, were manufactured up to 1943.

These jeans have a crotch rivet and a unique tag. The tag is made from horse or cowhide with the fur still intact. A tag placed near the inside middle of the waistband reads, "Union Made Sanforized Lee" in red-and-gold writing. At that time, the symbol on the back pockets was similar to that of the Levi's. The donut-hole buttons have one of three designs: leaves, "Union Made," or "Lee Cowboy."

Pricing of Lee buckle backs is the same as Levi's buckle backs.

EARLY RIVET.

CROTCH RIVET.

FUR TAG. Artist's rendition.

WAIST TAG.

TOP DONUT-HOLE BUTTON.

3 MANUFACTURED FROM 1943–1945

The second generation of Lee jeans is called Lee cowboy jeans without the buckle back. These jeans are exactly like Lee cowboy jeans, except for the missing buckle back and its changed back tag.

These jeans still have a Levi-like insignia on the back pockets. The woven tag near the inside center of the waistband remained the same, but the back tag is a more traditional leather without fur. The donut-hole buttons most likely have "Lee Cowboy" written upon them. Pricing is similar to Levi's World War II-era denim.

SHEARED TAG:
Lee's second-generation leather tag made a change; it lost its fur.

LOOK-ALIKE POCKET:
Lee's stitching closely resembles Levi's.

INSIDE OF OUTER SEAM:

4 1950s LEE PANTS

First manufactured in 1945, were the first to sport Lee's pocket symbol. Two different legends explain the origin of Lee's symbol. One legend relates that the symbol resembles a horse's mouth. Another legend says that the symbol represents a lazy "s." Before Lee's own symbol, the stitching on the back pocket was similar to that of Levi's. In addition, a red tag appears in the inside center of the waistband and a hairless waist tag reads only "Lee."

Pricing is similar to Levi's 501XX leather-tag series.

LATER RIVET:
Lee included their name from 1945.

LATER BUTTON:
Its name was added to buttons.

LEE'S LOGO:
This logo may represent a horse's mouth or a lazy "s."

POCKET TAG:
If this tag is intact, the exact manufacturing year can be known.

5 1960s LEES

The first to have a registered trademark symbol "®" as part of the Lee back tag. The red-and-gold tag on the back middle of the waist was moved to the hip, and the colors were changed to white and gold. These are priced similar to Levi's big E series.

6 IN THE LATE 1960s AND 1970s

Lee made a Lot No. 200 clothing line, which followed the 101 line. The last of the vintage Lee jeans from the sixties and seventies have the "®" and the "M. R." symbols on the back tag. These are priced similarly to Levi's red lines.

LEE'S LATE SIXTIES AND SEVENTIES TAG:
Lee added two letters to its tag of this era: M. R. This tag is still used today.

WRANGLER JEANS:

In 1904, a work-wear company, Blue Bell Overall, was established in North Carolina. Around 1925, the company was bought by another company and became Blue Bell Company. After many mergers, Blue Bell became the biggest work-wear company in the world.

During World War II, Blue Bell manufactured pants, jackets, military pants, and clothes for soldiers. The company prospered. After the war, in 1946, Blue Bell started manufacturing Wrangler jeans for cowboys and people who loved rodeos.

1 THE OLDEST VINTAGE WRANGLER JEANS WERE FIRST MANUFACTURED IN 1947.

These jeans, model No. 11MW, were produced through the 1950s. This is after both Levi and Lee started producing jeans; therefore, Wrangler has no buckle-back generation. Referred to as firsts, these jeans are distinguished by the leather tag on the right back pocket. The tag is placed at a different location than Levi and Lee—at the lip of the back pocket.

The rivets on the back of 11MWs are unique to Wrangler and have no lettering. The 11MW's back-pocket insignia is similar to Levi's. Lee and Wrangler insignias looked like Levi insignias when they were first produced. Legend has it that Levi Strauss sued the mimicking companies, and eventually Lee and Wrangler changed their insignias to what they are today.

Some Wranglers had different designs on the leather tags. For example, bullets and planes were pictured on the tag. Later, the tag was decorated with cowboys. Jeans with interesting and timely graphics are similar in price to World War II Levi's, depending on the condition.

This is a member of the XX generation.

2 WRANGLER'S "BIG E" GENERATION.

The Wrangler tag became plastic and acquired the registered trademark symbol "®" in 1964. The words "Blue Bell," written inside the bell, is stamped on the tag. Although the rivets are the same, the stitching on the back pocket changed to a Wrangler "W."

These pants have a "Blue Bell" label sewn on the back of the fly with the size and the word, "Sanforized." The main identifying characteristics to remember about this generation is the blue bell. This symbol is not found in any other generation of vintage Wrangler.

3 IN THE EARLY SEVENTIES

Wrangler discontinued the blue bell. The tag merely says "Wrangler" and has a registered trademark ®. The tag in the crotch area no longer has the blue bell symbol. 1970s jeans are part of the red-line generation. The white-woven label on today's nonvintage Wranglers is vertical.

LEVI'S JACKETS

1 TWO-POCKET JACKETS:

First-generation vintage jackets have two pockets. Like red lines, these jackets are single stitched or double stitched. Single-stitched jackets, stitched with cotton thread, are older than double-stitched jackets, stitched with nylon thread, and therefore more valuable.

Nylon single stitch has the same value as double stitch.

SINGLE OR DOUBLE STITCHED:

You can determine the difference between single- or double-stitch jackets by looking near the bottom button.

2 BIG E SERIES:

The next series of jackets were produced simultaneously. Each lot number indicates a slight jacket variation.

TWO-POCKET BIG E JACKETS:

The next stage of vintage jackets features a capital E on the red pocket tag.

LINED JACKETS:

All categories of Levi's denim jackets also come in a lined variety. At printing time, lined jackets aren't in as high a demand as unlined jackets. Lined jackets are still of some value. Make sure you include them in your vintage-jacket search.

LOT 557 SHORT TORSO: A popular style in Japan.

LOT 558 LONG TORSO: Popular in other areas; Japanese prefer 557s.

LOT 559 LINED JACKET: Not popular at this time.

3 507XX:

This stage of jackets has silver buttons with pleats on either side. Dealers refer to these jackets as "seconds." A Lot No. 517 indicates a lined jacket.

TWO TAGS:
507XXs can have a paper tag or a leather tag. Look for the words "Every Garment Guaranteed."

PLEATS AND SILVER BUTTONS:

4 507BXX:

The "B" in the lot number indicates that this jacket is a boy's size. Although the 507XX is vintage, youth sizes are not as valuable as adult sizes.

5 506XX:

Referred to as "firsts" by dealers, this jacket phase is distinguished by a single front pocket. Back buckles and bronze buckle clasps, along with pocket and cuff rivets, set the 506XX jacket apart.

6 OLDER FIRSTS:

An older 506XX can be distinguished by its buckle back, which is crafted in silver instead of bronze. The silver clasp also indicates a more valuable jacket.

7 DONUT HOLES:

Jackets with donut-hole buttons are the last stage of vintage Levi jackets. Donut-hole jackets can also be identified by the four buttons found on the front and the missing flap above the front pocket. Donut-hole variations distinguish a jacket's age. Most donut holes have ivy embossed on the buttons. Older and more valuable donut holes have "Levi Strauss" written on them.

LEGEND OF THE CLOTH:

According to a myth that has circulated throughout time, Levi Strauss used materials of different qualities in his production of clothing. Much like the companies who sell irregular clothing for reduced prices today, Strauss sold clothes made of lower-quality material at a discount. This lesser-quality material is supposedly indicated by a white, cloth tag. However, a cloth tag does not lower the value of a vintage item today. Both grades are valuable.

LEE JACKETS:

Lee jackets have three styles of pocket tags. Two of the tags are used on vintage jackets. The only marking on the oldest tag is "LEE." On the second vintage tag, a trademark symbol ® was added. On nonvintage tags, additional letters, "m. r.," appear below the trademark sign.

1950s LEE:

Plain styles were common in the fifties. Notice that Lee stitched only its name. Items bearing this tag are considered older-vintage Lee.

1960s LEE:

As competition increased, Lee began to protect its trademark and added a ®. Items with this tag are still vintage but are worth less than fifties Lee.

1970s AND BEYOND:

In the 1970s, Lee added an "M. R." to its tags. Items with this tag aren't considered vintage unless accompanied by a 101J tag.

1 1930S TO 1945:

Lee's first cowboy jacket was manufactured around the thirties. This one-pocket jacket came with a buckle back. The buttons have "Union Made" imprinted upon them, and the neck tag is white with blue-and-red writing. The pocket tag simply reads "Lee." These jackets are worth more than Levi jackets from the same time period—Lee produced less.

2 1945 TO EARLY 1950S:

The second generation of Lee jackets, 101J, also are referred to as Lee Cowboy jackets. "Lee Cowboy" is written upon the buttons. These jackets have two pockets and no buckle-back. The square neck tag is red-and-gold and reads "Union Made Lee Sanforized."
The red and gold tag reflects the fifties time period, as does Levi's first and second jackets.

3 1955 TO 1962:

The jacket tag of this era reads "Union Made Lee Sanforized Lot 101J Design Patent." The tag's writing is red and gold and has more information than the previous tag. Buttons read "Lee Rider." This tag had two versions: one that was stitched around the edges and another tag that was triangular-shaped and attached from the top. The triangle tag is harder to find and of greater value. These jackets are from the same time period as Levi's second jacket.

4 1962-1970:

This tag is white and gold. The major difference in this jacket is the pocket tag. Lee adopted the registered trademark symbol ®. Gold and white reflects the same time period as Levi's big E jackets.

5 101LJs:

Manufactured at the same time as 101Js. The "L" stands for "lined." This jacket is referred to as "Storm Rider." Changes in this line of jackets took place the same time as 101Js.

6 EARLY 1970S:

The black-and-gold tag is less cluttered and reads "Lee union made."

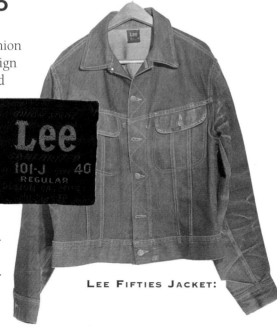

LEE FIFTIES JACKET:

WRANGLER JACKETS:

First and second Wrangler jackets come in lined versions and youth sizes. Youth sizes can be identified by the straight pocket insignia (no "W" stitching). Wrangler jackets produced after seconds have little value.

FRONT PLEATS

1 FIRSTS:

The first jackets, originally manufactured in the forties, include pleats down the front, tucked together by stitched dots, and two buckles in the back.

Wrangler jackets were preferred by cowboys at the time because they were designed better. For example, elastic straps were built inside to help shoulders move.

HIDDEN SHOULDER STRAP

BACK BUCKLE

2 SECONDS:

Seconds were manufactured in the fifties and continued until the late seventies. Unique to all denim jackets are the three pockets found on Wrangler seconds. Two pockets are located on the bottom of the jacket, and the other is located on the upper-left chest area.

Another unique aspect to seconds is the zipper and added elastic in the back.

All vintage Wrangler jackets have the Blue Bell mark. In fact, anything with that mark has a chance of being valuable.

Seconds have been made in many different colors, including red, brown, blue, and others.

WORK WEAR:

Levi and Lee made overalls before they made traditional jeans. Although overalls can be old, they aren't as valuable as Lee and Levi pants. Overalls can be worth up to almost $1,800.

BUCKLE-BACK GENERATION:

Overalls/coveralls can be identified by their buttons. A Levi donut-hole button has ivy embossing or "Levi Strauss" imprinted on it. Lee overalls have "Union All" written on the donut-hole buttons. Good-condition overalls are hard to find because they were worn while working.

LEE COVERALLS.

DOUBLE XX GENERATION:

As Lee and Levi continued to make overalls, Lee added two jackets to its work-wear line. Lot numbers for Lee jackets are 91J and 191J. These jackets can also be identified by a house silhouette on the tag. Lee 91J can be worth up to $230, and 191J jackets can be worth up to $185.

J. C. Penney, Payday, Sears, Big Smith, and other brands of overalls may be considered vintage work wear and can be worth up to $180.

BIG E GENERATION:

Overalls and Lee jackets continued to be manufactured in this final generation of vintage work wear. They still carry some value but are worth only up to $80.

LEE 191J

FIRST-GRADE DENIM

After you know which defects to look for, start grading your own jeans. On the first-grade jeans pictured below, notice that different fades don't downgrade any of the jeans

PERFECT FIRST:
A dark color and no holes or stains equals a perfect pair.

FADED FIRST:
The thighs are highly faded, but the fabric has not worn through.

WORN FIRST:
The pocket area is well worn, but no holes have developed—judged a first.

WORN-SEAT FIRST:
The seat area has seen many chairs, but not enough to make a hole.

SECOND-GRADE DENIM

STAIN

POCKET HOLE   KNEE HOLE

THIRD-GRADE DENIM

SMALL POCKET HOLE

LARGE STAIN

HOLES

KNEE HOLE

RAGGED HEM

FOURTH-GRADE DENIM

LARGE CROTCH HOLE   PEGGED LEGS

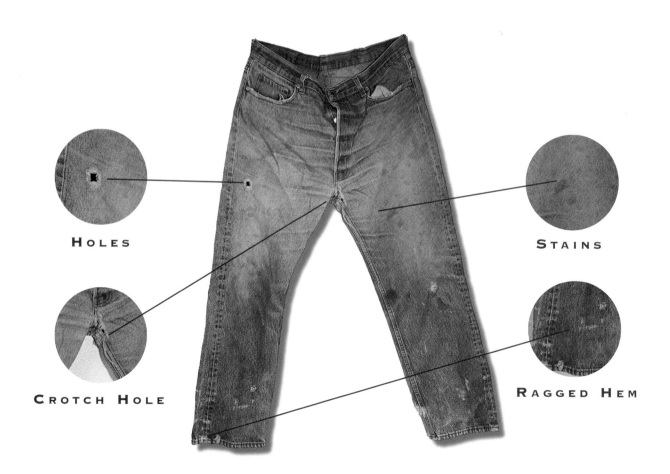

HOLES   STAINS

CROTCH HOLE   RAGGED HEM

HOW TO GRADE USED LEVI'S JACKETS:

Grading Levi's jackets is similar to grading jeans. Look at the same characteristics: size, fade, holes, patches, and stains. A few differences do exist. Levi's jackets are graded as firsts, seconds, or thirds. Often jackets are decorated, and these alterations are taken into consideration.

1 VINTAGE:

All vintage Levi jackets have two pockets. Nonvintage jackets have four pockets.

2 SIZE:

Ideal sizes are between 36 and 42. Anything smaller or larger will lower the jacket one grade. The jacket picture above appears to be a first-grade item but isn't because of its size—18.

3 HOLES AND STAINS:

Hole location is not as critical for jackets as for jeans. The size and quantity, however, are factors to remember when grading a jacket. Stains and holes follow the same rules that apply to jeans.

FIRST GRADE:
No holes allowed.

SECOND GRADE:
These jackets can have one or two dime-sized holes. Check the cuffs and collar where holes are often hidden.

THIRD GRADE:
Thirds can have holes no larger than a half dollar.

4 PATCHES:

You may find more patches on jackets than you do on jeans. Owners decorate jackets, and many use patches. When grading jackets, look for patch remnants and patches that were used to repair holes and for patch remnants.

FIRST GRADE:
No patches or patch remnants.

SECOND GRADE:
No patches are allowed for second grades. Remnants of patches are fine if there are no holes.

THIRD GRADE:
Patches and their remnants are allowed for third grades.

5 FADE:

Fading characteristics for jackets and jeans are identical. Any fade will do except for stonewashed; the jacket still must be the original Levi blue. To determine the original jacket color, lift the pocket flap. The color usually doesn't fade in that area.

6 DECORATIONS:

Grading jackets with decorations is difficult. Sometimes decorations enhance the jacket and increase its value, and other decorations detract from jacket appearance and lower its value. Use your best judgement, and follow these guidelines when grading decorated jackets:

A. Is the decoration in good taste, free of vulgarity?

B. Are the decorations attractive? Are they fastened with care?

C. Is the decoration top quality?

D. Has the decoration left the jacket free of holes or tears?

If you answered yes to these questions, most likely the decorations enhance jacket value. If any question was answered no, most likely the decorations cause lower jacket value— lowered by at least one grade.

VINTAGE EXPRESS

Once you have read *Vintage Denim* and are ready to start finding vintage, you need to know how to exchange your vintage for cash.

Farley Enterprises has made this process simple. Depending on your items, you may be able to send your items through Federal Express at little or no cost to you. To determine if your vintage items are eligible for the reduced Federal Express rate, call (801) 224-3317. Using Federal Express will get your vintage to our headquarters fast. We will grade your vintage and send your money.

• **Farley Enterprises will send a payment for your vintage using two methods:**

1 **We will send you a check through the U.S. mail**—standard delivery — within one day from receiving your vintage shipment.

2 **For a $10 service charge, Farley Enterprises will Federal Expresss your check** within one day from receiving your vintage.

We, at Farley Enterprises, are excited for you and your new business opportunity. Don't hesitate to start finding vintage. The sooner you find vintage and send it to us, the sooner we can send your profit. Good luck!

Farley Enterprises
625 North 1200 West
Orem, Utah 84057
(801) 224-3317 fax (801) 224-3133

Becoming our partner in the pursuit of vintage clothing is quite simple. Everything included in the subscription is yours for only $100 per year?

Subscribe to *Vintage Partner* magazine and receive four quarterly issues, plus:

☞ A partnership through the internet
☞ *Vintage Partner* staff will assist you in getting online
☞ questions answered quickly through e-mail
☞ access to restricted areas of *Vintage Partner* online
☞ updated pricing and shopping lists
☞ One free Fax Appraisal
☞ One free auction submission

Vintage Partner magazine

is filled with valuable information for the American vintage clothing seller and the Japanese vintage clothing consumer. *Vintage Partner* is divided into two sections: half is directed toward the American public and the other half is for the Japanese public. *Vintage Partner* features departments such as success stories, trends, denim, and military in every issue. Through joining this partnership, you will be able to communicate through the internet. Get on the information superhighway and let the staff at *Vintage Partner* answer your questions. Through the internet, you will receive updated pricing and shopping lists, access to restricted areas of *Vintage Partner* online and questions answered quickly through e-mail.

1 **Send your $100 subscription fee.**

2 **Connect to the internet.** Use the updated price and shopping lists to find your vintage. Get any questions answered through e-mail.

3 **Find vintage.** Use the information in *Vintage Denim* to find the most desirable items.

4 **Send vintage to Farley Enterprises.** Send your vintage and you will receive cash!
Prices are based upon size, condition, color, current fashion trends, and the exchange rate. Any variations may change the price. Prices valid at printing time.

	Item	Price
	Vintage Levi's Jeans	
Red Lines	Double stitch	$100
	Single stitch	$150
	Single stitch; two tone	$175
	Big E	$460
501XX	"Lot 501XX"	$750
	Hidden rivets	$852
	Paper tag	$825
	Paper tag; "Every Garment Guaranteed"	$1,015
	Leather tag; "Every Garment Guaranteed"	$1,470
Donut Hole	WWIIXX: painted pocket	$2,235
	"Levi Strauss & Co."	$2,235
	Leaf logo	$2,235
	One-sided white stitching	$2,235
	Buckle-Backs	$3,410
	Vintage Lee Jeans	
	Lee Cowboy: buckle-back	$4,588
	Lee Cowboy: no buckle-back	$1,235
	Lee fifties pants	$1,115
	Lee sixties pants	$290
	Lee late-sixties and seventies pants	$190
	Vintage Wrangler Jeans	
First	11MW	$790
	Graphics on tag	$790
	Plastic Blue Bell tag	$215
	1970s pants	$100
	Vintage Levi's Jackets	
Two Pocket	Double-stitch	$30
	Double-stitch; lined	$20
	Single-stitch	$75
	Single-stitch; lined	$30
Big E	Two-Pocket Jacket	$190
	Two-Pocket Jacket; lined	$90
	557 Jacket	$575
	558 Jacket	$460
	559 Jacket	$460
	507XX Jacket (Second)	$1,050
	517XX Jacket (Second)	$1,050
	506XX Jacket (First)	$2,225
	506XX Jacket (First); lined	$2,225
	Older First: silver buckle	$2,515
	Donut Holes, ivy buttons	$2,515
	Donut hole, Levi Strauss & Co.	$2,515

	Item	Price
	Lee Jackets	
	First Cowboy: buckle-back	$5,880
	Cowboy Jacket	$1,635
	Rider: Lot 101J; square tag	$990
	Rider: Lot 101J; triangle tag	$1,165
	1960s Work Jacket	$160
	1960s: gold-and-white tag	$205
	101LJ Jacket: Storm Rider	$185
	1970s, black-and-gold tag	$110
	Wrangler Jackets	
	First Jacket	$930
	First Jacket; lined	$790
	Second Jacket	$320
	Second Jacket; lined	$282
	Work Wear	
Overalls/Coveralls	Levi: Buckle-Back Era	$1,790
	Lee: Buckle-Back Era	$1,550
	Levi: XX Era	$185
	Lee: XX Era	$185
	Lee: Big E Era	$80
	Big Smith Overalls	$180
	Payday Overalls	$180
	J. C. Penny Overalls	$180
	Sears Overalls	$180
	Lee 91J Jacket	$230
	Lee 191J Jacket	$185
	Advertisements	
	Levi's Dance Tonight Advertisement	$1,000
	Levi's Barber Shop Advertisement	$1,000
	Levi's Rodeo Advertisement	$1,000
	Levi's Press on the Run Advertisement	$1,000
	Wrangler Advertisement	$600
	Lee metal banners	$200
	Denim Levi Western Customs	$1,600
	Denim Levi Solid Comfort Advertisement	$1,600
	Denim Wrangler Advertisement	$700

As classic as an old wagon, denim has
been a part of our history for a
hundred years, and photo
albums of the future
no doubt will hold
pictures of kids
in denim
jeans.

REMEMBERING OUR JEANS
DEJA BLUE

America is a country "forever in blue jeans," as Neil Diamond sang in a song extolling youth and denim. We had to give up our teddy bears, our letter sweaters, and class rings but never our jeans. No matter that Ronald Reagan wears jeans or that middle-aged Americans buy relaxed-fit jeans for their aging bodies, jeans will always stay young. Blue jeans won't ever become old people's clothes no matter how old the wearers get, and they will always remind us what it was like to be young and carefree.

FLYER

The sixties are alive and well in the nineties as the fascination with that decade shows in today's fashion.

Whenever we pull on a pair of blue jeans, there is a link to our past—a past that remembers holes in knees, sticky ironed-on patches, and big cuffs full of dirt and grass; or the summer rite of cutting off last year's jeans, shopping for new, dark-blue, stiff jeans to go back to school, sitting in the tub to shrink those new jeans tight, cutting them off to fray the cuffs, and pegging them to get them tapered so tight they had to be turned inside out to get them off. We remember how good our jeans felt and, as we got older, how good someone else's jeans felt, unless of course we were trying to wrestle them out of their jeans. Jeans lured teens with their lurid tightness and mocked us with that same tightness that made them impossible to remove with any degree of suaveness. Fighting off a cotton-cocoon of shrunk-to-fit

denim just wasn't sexy. Undressing for sex always seemed so sexy in movies, but wrestling a mate out of skintight jeans was definitely not sexy and, at best, was comical. Looking sexy in tight jeans was important, but if spontaneous sex was desired, baggy pants worked best.

Maybe that had something to do with wearing loose bell-bottoms as Americans hit the mid-sixties, the era of "free love" and the sexual revolution. We will remember those days too, every time we pull on our blue jeans. We will remember painting our jeans with antiwar slogans, tearing out the seams to add a flowered or paisley insert, the cuffs fraying from dragging the ground, the dirty bare feet of summer sticking out of the bottoms. We will remember the seventies and designer denim—tight, pressed, polyester-stretchy, disco denim. We will remember being sent home from school, our jeans in flagrant disregard for the discipline of the dress code. We will remember the eighties with scrubbed, brushed, colored, acid-washed, bleached, battered, batiked, stonewashed, ripped, torn, gashed, and slashed denim. We will remember tight new cowboy boots and a new pair of Wranglers as we boot-scooted into the nineties and perhaps our first computer fit, robotic tailor-made Levi's. We someday may even remember first becoming aware of vintage denim and smiling as we sold our old jeans for big bucks. We may someday remember paying big bucks for jeans our fathers or grandfathers might have worn or our mothers might have thrown out.

Will those who pay many yen, pounds, marks, rubles, rupees, drachmas, francs, and other currencies for old American jeans ever feel for them what Americans did growing up in their good ol' jeans? Could the buyers ever remember, like Americans do, jeans being soaked and stiff with snow because of foolishly scorning ski pants in favor of old Levi's? Might they remember stapling their short, tight jeans of junior high school to the top of their roughout suede cowboy boots? Or will they remember their moms' sewing a yellow cloth stripe down the side so they could pretend they were a cavalry soldier playing cowboys and Indians, or sewing a peace-sign patch on the rear of their best, ragged pair of sky-blue worn jeans, or a big brother stapling under the cuffs of their long jeans because rolling them up looked like a farmer? Perhaps. Perhaps not. But what they will have is their very own remembrances of their jeans. No matter where they came from, who wore them before, how much was paid for them, how rare they might be, how in or out of fashion they might be, jeans will always be full of memories for all nationalities.

Jeans always remind us of softness, comfort, warmth, youth, and a sentimental connection to our pasts. Our jeans don't ask much of us, maybe a trip through the washer now and then, but they give us so much. It's satisfying to know that old jeans have gained a reverence and an appreciation in the world of vintage denim. Somehow it seems a sign of respect that jeans should go on to a new life instead of becoming a paint rag. That dubious honor should be reserved for stuffy, uncomfortable dress clothing. We can't wait to peel off the tightness and formality of a business suit or church clothes and get into our jeans. Putting on a pair of jeans is like coming home. And no matter where Americans go, we can take that bit of home with us.

An advertising slogan says, "Cotton: The Fabric of Our Lives," and those who wear cotton denim know that to be true. Our lives are woven into our jeans—a blue cotton canvas of memories that offers a continuity of comfort, a link to the past and to one another.

R E S O U R C E S

Finding, buying, and selling vintage denim can be an exciting treasure hunt or frustrating wild-goose chase. We hope this book has taken some of the mystery out of your search, unveiled a few secrets, and pointed you in the right direction. If you need some advice or more information about the objects, people, or places in this book, please use the following source list.

V I N T A G E - D E N I M   D E A L E R S

Jack Dovan
American Classics
7368 Melrose Avenue
Los Angeles, CA 90046

Barbara Dryden
Mr. Higgin's Second Chance
612 South Higgins Avenue
Missoula, MT 59801
(406) 721-6446

John Farley
Farley Enterprises
625 North 1200 West
Orem, UT 84057
(801) 224-3130

Theodore Kyriazis
Jethro Classic Wear
9546 West Pico Boulevard
Los Angeles, CA 90046
(310) 278-9683

David Little
PRAIRIE
2765 Osceola Street
Denver, CO 80212
(303) 458-5779
1-800-665-4237 (Code 3837)

Nihat Ulusoy
American Vintage
Worn Out West
645 North Martel
Los Angeles, CA 90036
(213) 653-5645

Ron and Cindy Wright
BOSS Unlimited
301 East 57th Avenue
Denver, CO 80216
(303) 296-BOSS
1-800-807-2677 (BOSS)
1-800-733-6461 (Denim 1) After Hours

DENIM MANUFACTURER ARCHIVES

Levi Strauss & Company
Levi's Plaza
1155 Battery Street
P.O. Box 7215
San Francisco, CA 94120
Lynne Downey, Historian

LEE Archival Committee
Claudia Broaddus
9001 West 67th
Merriam, KS 66202
(913) 384-4000 (ext. 220)

WRANGLER Archives
Linda Hand
400 North Elm Street
Greensboro, NC 27401
(910) 332-3402

PRISON BLUES
THE BIG HOUSE
P.O. Box 6773
Beaverton, OR 97007
(503) 645-7107
1-800-597-7472

COWBOY AND WESTERN COLLECTIBLES

David Little
PRAIRIE
2765 Osceola Street
Denver, CO 80212
(303) 458-5779

Gary Schneckloth
14479 West 32nd Avenue
Denver, CO 80212

MUSEUMS

Roy Rogers and Dale Evans Museum
15650 Seneca Road
Victorville, CA 92393
(619) 243-4547

Gene Autry Western Heritage Museum
4700 Western Heritage Way
Los Angeles, CA 90027-1426
(213) 667-2000

OLD RECORDS AND JUKEBOXES

David Metcalfe
4025 Grove Street
Denver, CO 80212
(303) 480-9984

VINTAGE MOTORCYCLES AND VEHICLES

The Motor Ranch
John Sawazhki
451 East 58th Avenue
Box 113
Denver, CO 80216
(303) 295-1011

The Forney Transportation Museum
1416 Platte Street
Denver, CO 80202
(303) 433-3643

Gallery of Cars
Kendrick Fidler
1144 Broadway
Denver, CO 80110
(303) 762-8450

Rocky Mountain Harley-Davidson
Vinnie Terranova
4204 South Broadway
Denver, CO 80110
(303) 762-8450

Harley-Davidson denim motorcycle, courtesy of *Big Twin* magazine.

P H O T O   C R E D I T S

All photographs by Larry Bond except as noted:

David Little photographs, pages 20, 31, 32, 42, 43, 52, 53, 56, 60, 74, 76, 86, 87, 96, 98, 112, 114.

H. D. Lee Co., pages 22, 24, 33, 34, 35, 40, 46, 47, 50, 89.

Walker Evans photographs, pages 37, 38, 39.

Marilyn Monroe and Clark Gable, page 61, courtesy of Magnum Photos.

page 62, courtesy of Wrangler and *Newsweek*.

page 63, Marilyn Monroe courtesy of Magnum Photos.

pages 51 and 64, courtesy of Roy Rogers Jr. and the Roy Rogers and Dale Evans Museum.

page 58, James Dean, courtesy of Magnum Photos.

page 65, from *Look* magazine.

pages 72-73, Jane Fonda and Robert Redford, courtesy of Magnum Photos.

page 75, design by Andy Warhol.

page 82, photo of Bruce Springsteen album.

page 84, Daryl Hannah, courtesy of *You* magazine.

page 92, catalog, courtesy of Cheyenne Outfitters.

pages 120–143, all photographs, courtesy of *Vintage Partner* magazine.

page 151, Harley-Davidson denim motorcycle, courtesy of *Big Twin* magazine.

A special thanks to John Farley and his staff at *Vintage Partner* magazine for their creation of the pricing guide and for all other assistance in the compilation of *Vintage Denim.*

DAVID LITTLE, left, a vintage clothing buyer, is a freelance writer who has written articles for the *Denver Post,* the Associated Press, The Buffalo Bill Historical Center, where he was Public Relations Director, and for many business and consumer organizations. He lives in Denver.

LARRY BOND, right, formerly a staff photographer for the May Company in Southern California, is now a freelance fashion photographer working in the Denver area.